# Java From Zero

*The Complete Guide With Code Examples and Exercises to Become a Professional*

Scott Brandt

## © Copyright 2023 - All rights reserved.

The content contained within this book may not be reproduced, duplicated or transmitted without direct written permission from the author or the publisher.

Under no circumstances will any blame or legal responsibility be held against the publisher, or author, for any damages, reparation, or monetary loss due to the information contained within this book, either directly or indirectly.

Legal Notice:

This book is copyright protected. It is only for personal use. You cannot amend, distribute, sell, use, quote or paraphrase any part, or the content within this book, without the consent of the author or publisher.

Disclaimer Notice:

Please note the information contained within this document is for educational and entertainment purposes only. All effort has been executed to present accurate, up to date, reliable, complete information. No warranties of any kind are declared or implied. Readers acknowledge that the author is not engaged in the rendering of legal, financial, medical or professional advice. The content within this book has been derived from various sources. Please consult a licensed professional before attempting any techniques outlined in this book.

By reading this document, the reader agrees that under no circumstances is the author responsible for any losses, direct or indirect, that are incurred as a result of the use of the information contained within this document, including, but not limited to, errors, omissions, or inaccuracies.

# Table of Contents

## Contents

Table of Contents ........................................................................................... 3
Introduction .................................................................................................. 10
    Where Is Java Used? ................................................................................ 11
    Where Can I Work? .................................................................................. 13
    The Benefits ............................................................................................. 14
    What Will Change? .................................................................................. 15
    About the Author .................................................................................... 16
Chapter 1: Setting Up Your Development Environment ............................. 17
    Tools for Java Development .................................................................... 17
        The Java Development Kit ................................................................ 17
        An Integrated Development Environment ...................................... 18
        Build Tool and Dependency Manager .............................................. 19
    Setting Up Your Development Environment .......................................... 21
        Installing the JDK ............................................................................. 21
        Installing the IDE .............................................................................. 23
        Installing Build Tool and Dependency Manager ............................. 24
    Summary ................................................................................................. 25
Chapter 2: Setting Up Your Own Java Project ............................................. 26
    How to Set Up Your Own Java Project .................................................... 26
        Creating a Project ............................................................................. 26
        Running Your Project ....................................................................... 29
        Debugging Your Project ................................................................... 30
        Distributing Your Project ................................................................. 32
    Summary ................................................................................................. 34
Chapter 3: Creating Your First Java Program .............................................. 35
    Adding a Package .................................................................................... 35
    Adding a Main Class ................................................................................ 36

Writing Your First Java Program ................................................................. 38

Running Your Code ...................................................................................... 38

Adding a Second Class ................................................................................ 39

Running Multiple Programs ........................................................................ 40

Summary ....................................................................................................... 42

Chapter 4: Using Comments in Java ............................................................... 43

What Are Comments? .................................................................................. 43

How to Write Comments in Java ............................................................... 44

   Single-Line Comments ........................................................................... 44

   Multi-Line Comments ............................................................................ 45

   Documentation Comments ................................................................... 46

Using Comments .......................................................................................... 51

   Why Use Comments? .............................................................................. 51

   How NOT to Use Comments ................................................................ 52

   Tips for Using Comments Effectively ................................................. 53

Exercise .......................................................................................................... 55

Summary ....................................................................................................... 56

Chapter 5: Working With Variables and Data Types in Java ..................... 57

What Are Variables and Data Types? ....................................................... 57

Types of Variables ........................................................................................ 60

   Local Variables ........................................................................................ 60

   Instance Variables ................................................................................... 61

   Class Variables ........................................................................................ 62

Rules for Naming Variables in Java .......................................................... 64

More Information on Variables .................................................................. 65

   Variable Scope and Lifetime ................................................................. 65

   Mutable and Immutable Variables ...................................................... 67

Working With Data Types in Java ............................................................. 72

   The Eight Primitive Data Types in Java ............................................. 72

   How to Convert Between Data Types ................................................ 76

   Non-Primitive Data Types ..................................................................... 79

- Exercise ............................................................................................................. 81
- Summary ........................................................................................................... 83

## Chapter 6: Creating and Using Strings in Java ............................................. 84
- Creating Strings in Java ................................................................................. 85
- Using Strings in Java ..................................................................................... 86
- Exercises ........................................................................................................ 89
- Summary ........................................................................................................ 91

## Chapter 7: Using Arrays in Java ........................................................................ 92
- What Is an Array? .......................................................................................... 92
- How to Create an Array in Java ................................................................... 93
- How to Use an Array in Java ........................................................................ 93
- Exercise ........................................................................................................... 95
- Summary ......................................................................................................... 97

## Chapter 8: Using Operators and Decision-Making in Java ........................ 98
- Learning About Operators in Java and How to Use Them ..................... 98
  - Arithmetic Operators ................................................................................. 98
  - Assignment Operators ............................................................................. 100
  - Comparison or Relational Operators .................................................... 101
  - Logical Operators ..................................................................................... 102
  - Bitwise Operators ..................................................................................... 103
  - Misc Operators ......................................................................................... 104
- Decision-Making in Java ............................................................................ 104
  - If Statement ............................................................................................... 105
  - If-Else Statement ...................................................................................... 106
  - Else-if Statement ...................................................................................... 107
  - Switch Case Statement ........................................................................... 108
  - Miscellaneous Statements ...................................................................... 109
- Exercise ......................................................................................................... 109
- Summary ....................................................................................................... 111

## Chapter 9: Control Flow Statements ............................................................. 112
- All About Control Flow Statements .......................................................... 112

5

Types of Control Flow Statements ............................................................................ 112

Exercise ............................................................................................................................ 119

Summary ........................................................................................................................ 120

## Chapter 10: Creating Methods in Java ............................................................. 121

Methods in Java ........................................................................................................... 121

    Why Use Methods? ................................................................................................. 121

    How to Create Methods in Java ........................................................................... 122

Types of Methods in Java .......................................................................................... 124

The Basics of Methods in Java ................................................................................. 125

    Declaring a Method ................................................................................................ 126

    Invoking a Method .................................................................................................. 127

    Returning a Value From a Method ..................................................................... 128

Advanced Methods in Java ....................................................................................... 128

Exercise ............................................................................................................................ 131

Summary ........................................................................................................................ 133

## Chapter 11: Object-Oriented Programming in Java .................................... 134

What Is OOP? ................................................................................................................ 134

    Pillars ........................................................................................................................... 135

    Concepts .................................................................................................................... 136

    Difference in Paradigm .......................................................................................... 137

The Benefits of OOP ................................................................................................... 139

    Troubleshooting ...................................................................................................... 139

    Increased Productivity .......................................................................................... 140

    Reusability ................................................................................................................. 140

    Criticism of OOP ..................................................................................................... 140

Getting Started With OOP in Java .......................................................................... 141

Using Encapsulation to Improve Code Quality .................................................. 143

Implementing Polymorphism in Java and its Relation to Inheritance ....... 145

Exercise ............................................................................................................................ 148

Summary ........................................................................................................................ 150

## Chapter 12: Application of Inheritance, Interface, and Extension in Java ............ 151

Inheritance in Java ........................................................................................ 151
   Types of Inheritance ................................................................................ 152
   Benefits of Using Inheritance .................................................................. 155
   Disadvantages of Inheritance .................................................................. 156
   Simple Example of Inheritance in Java .................................................. 156
   How to Write a Main Method to Instantiate and Use Objects From Both Classes 160
   Exercise ..................................................................................................... 163
Using Interfaces With Java ......................................................................... 166
   What Are Interfaces? ............................................................................... 166
   How to Work With Interfaces ................................................................. 168
   The Disadvantage of Interfaces .............................................................. 169
   Why Use Interfaces? ................................................................................ 170
   Using Interfaces to Create Multiple Inheritance ................................... 172
   Using Interfaces to Create Hybrid Inheritance ..................................... 174
   Exercise ..................................................................................................... 175
Extending the Java Language ..................................................................... 178
   Basic Concepts of Extending the Java Language ................................. 178
Applying the Concepts of Extending the Java Language ........................ 183
   How to Extend the Java Language Using Interfaces ........................... 183
   How to Extend the Java Language Using Abstract Classes ................ 184
   How to Extend the Java Language Using Inner Classes ..................... 186
   How to Extend the Java Language Using Inheritance ........................ 188
   Summary .................................................................................................. 190
Chapter 13: Creating and Using Collections in Java ................................. 192
   The Java Collections Framework ........................................................... 192
   Common Operations on Collections ...................................................... 195
   Creating and Using Collections .............................................................. 196
      Creating an ArrayList .......................................................................... 196
      Creating a HashMap ............................................................................ 197
      Adding Elements to a Collection ........................................................ 199
      Iterating Over a Collection ................................................................. 200

- Removing Elements From a Collection ................................................................. 205
- Autoboxing and Unboxing .................................................................................... 207
- Exercise .................................................................................................................. 210
- Summary ................................................................................................................ 214

# Chapter 14: Troubleshooting, Debugging, and Handling Errors and Exceptions in Java ................................................................................................................... 215

- Basic Errors and Exceptions ................................................................................... 216
  - Exceptions ........................................................................................................... 217
  - Errors ................................................................................................................... 217
  - Don't Stress If You Find an Error! ...................................................................... 223
- Exception Handling Keywords in Java .................................................................. 223
  - Try ........................................................................................................................ 224
  - Catch .................................................................................................................... 225
  - Finally .................................................................................................................. 226
  - Throw ................................................................................................................... 226
  - Throws ................................................................................................................. 227
  - One More Example ............................................................................................. 228
- Troubleshooting and Debugging Your Java Programs ......................................... 229
  - Troubleshooting and Debugging Java Programs .............................................. 230
  - Tips for Troubleshooting and Debugging Java Programs ................................ 231
- Summary ................................................................................................................ 233

# Chapter 15: Reading and Writing Files in Java ................................................. 234

- Introduction to Reading and Writing Files in Java ............................................... 234
  - Why Read and Write Files? ................................................................................ 234
  - How to Read and Write Files in Java ................................................................. 235
- Creating and Writing Files in Java ........................................................................ 236
- Reading Files in Java ............................................................................................. 239
- Exercise .................................................................................................................. 242
- Summary ................................................................................................................ 245

# Chapter 16: Using Databases in Java ................................................................. 246

- How Databases Are Used in Java ......................................................................... 246

- Creating a Database in Java ............................................................. 247
  - How to Use a Simple Database ..................................................... 249
  - Creating Tables and Fields in the Database .................................... 249
  - Inserting Data Into the Database ................................................... 252
- Advanced Database Concepts ........................................................... 254
  - Transactions .................................................................................. 254
  - Indexes ......................................................................................... 257
- Exercise ............................................................................................ 259
- Summary .......................................................................................... 264

# Chapter 17: Distributing Your Java Applications .................................. 265
- Distribution vs. Deployment .............................................................. 266
- How to Package and Distribute a Java Program ................................ 266
  - How to Package My Code ............................................................. 267
- How to Run a Java Program Once It's Been Distributed ..................... 269
- Summary .......................................................................................... 271

# Chapter 18: Tips and Tricks for Java Programming ............................... 272

# Conclusion ........................................................................................ 275

# References ........................................................................................ 277

# Introduction

*Code is like humor. When you have to explain it, it's bad.* –Cory House

If you were using a computer a decade ago, you might remember a time when you needed to update it often and, sometimes, an orange icon with a coffee cup asked you to "update Java." If you don't remember, all you need to know is that this used to be pretty common. One of the reasons for this is that Java was and still is among one the most used software by developers and corporations. Because of this, users are constantly receiving updates to the software as new features are released.

But you probably already know this, and knowing Java trivia is not the main reason you bought this book. You intend to *learn* Java and become a developer proficient in this coding language. Well, guess what? You have come to the right place. Maybe you are already a developer in another language that wants to increase your knowledge by learning a new one.

Or maybe you are looking for a career change, and Java was presented to you as one of the best languages to know. Or maybe you have tried learning it by yourself, but you have more questions than answers, and you need someone to guide you through the steps to clarify things.

No matter the reason, I can assure you have come to the right place. Here, we will start with the basics and progress into more complex themes regarding Java and what it means to code with it. I will provide tips and easy references to make your learning curve faster. Once you are done, you will see that Java has no mystery and can be a very straightforward language, enabling you to dive head-first into the market and start growing your career.

It helps that Java is one of the most popular programming languages. According to Veeraraghavan (2022), "Today, there are more than 3 billion devices running applications built with Java" (4. Java section), making it widely popular independent of the platform you are using. Whether it is Windows, Android, Mac, Linux, or any other, Java's versatility enables its application in several different areas—especially in the back end of common programs such as YouTube and Amazon.

While this should be sufficient motivation to start learning, you could still be worried that Java might become irrelevant with the growth of different languages, such as Python. Granted, other languages have gone to the top of the rank, and Java has been bumped down to the 6th most-used language among developers worldwide, according to a poll by Statista (2022). However, this does not mean that it has lost its relevance. Although it is being extensively debated (if you search Google for "relevance of Java programming language," you will get more than 600 million results), it is unlikely that it will go anywhere anytime soon.

## Where Is Java Used?

As one of the most popular programming languages in the world, Java quietly powers some of the largest websites and applications. You can get a sense of just how versatile it is as a language based on how it's used for web development, mobile development, desktop development, and more.

Some of the uses of Java in the market include:

- Web development for creating applications. Some of the largest websites in the world such as Amazon, eBay, and LinkedIn are built with Java (W3Techs, 2023).

- Mobile applications largely use Java as their main programming language. If you have an Android phone, you are using Java technology. The same goes if you are a Netflix or Tinder subscriber.

- Embedded systems, which are smaller computer systems within larger devices such as a car or an airplane, use Java. In the car, you will find it in the control system and the flight management system of an airplane. If you own a television, its setup is probably built on Java technology.

- Java is also used in science. Scientists use Java-based programs to solve complex scientific and mathematical problems. This includes the Mars Climate Simulator and the Cancer Cell Simulator programs.

- We couldn't leave out video games. Some of the most popular in recent years were built on Java, including Minecraft, Angry Birds, and Temple Run.

- If you think about the present age of computing, you will likely immediately think about the cloud. Cloud applications such as the Amazon Elastic Compute Cloud (EC2) and the Google App Engine were written in Java.

- Java is also used for processing large amounts of data, also known as big data. Applications that were written with the language include the Hadoop Distributed File System (HDFS) and the Apache Spark framework.

- If you think about what the future holds for technology, Java is certainly a part of it. Several artificial intelligence applications are written in Java. These include IBM Watson and Google DeepMind AlphaGo.

- Last but not least, we have blockchain applications. Blockchains are programs that run on a decentralized and distributed ledger and some of the most important, such as the Ethereum and the Hyperledger Fabric platforms, are written in Java.

It is safe to say that while Java has been playing a role in the technology market for at least 20+ years, based on the new technologies that are being developed and built with this programming language, it is unlikely to lose its relevance in the foreseeable future. This means that if you are thinking about investing in a career with Java, there is no reason not to start now. Many companies are constantly recruiting and looking for new talent in the market that can bring them solutions to optimize their services.

## Where Can I Work?

Java is one of the most in-demand programming languages, and programmers with expertise in Java can command high salaries. The salary is still attractive to many who, according to Glassdoor (2022), can earn an annual salary between $80,000 and $125,000, with an average of $99,500. This should be attractive enough to guarantee that new Java developers enter the market every day, added to the large number of companies that seem unlikely to change their back-end structures abruptly.

Some of the jobs that require Java knowledge are in software, web, and mobile development, and big data analytics. In addition to this, WebDev (2019) states that in a survey carried out by the U.S. Bureau of Labor Statistics, the demand for developers who know Java will increase by 20% by 2024. The path of a developer is usually the following: junior programmer, senior programmer, architect, then an IT manager. The last step would be to evolve into a chief technology officer (CTO) of an organization where you will need to apply management skills to the technical ones you already have.

Speaking of skills, do you know what are the ones needed to become a Java developer? The first and most important one is to have a problem-solving mindset that enjoys working with logic. Next, you should be familiar with popular Java development tools such as Eclipse, which we will mention later in this book, and IntelliJ IDEA.

Having prior knowledge of other languages is not essential—although if you do have some experience with object-oriented programming (OOP), you will likely have an advantage over others who have had no contact with it before. However, these are just some of the skills that are required and each company will request a different set of characteristics from their developers.

The required skill set will generally be available in the job descriptions you find. The most common way to find a job as a developer is to look for online job postings on specialized websites for programmers and also LinkedIn. Some companies, although they will post job vacancies on these pages, it is likely they will also ask you to register on their website.

This will be quite an advantage since organizations are constantly looking for new talent to fill in open positions and they generally look first into the talent that has shown an interest before in working for them.

Additionally, you can research companies that use Java technology and voluntarily register your resumé in the talent database. Another option is to call the human resources department to ask where you can send your resume to. Even if you do not have positive feedback on the first try, you can always ask them if they participate in job fairs in your region that you could attend.

These fairs are excellent to get to know recruiters and middle-management employees who will likely be conducting your interview process. Remember also to participate in networking events and spread the word that you are starting to look for a job as a Java developer. When you least expect it, someone you know can refer you to a position that requires new talent.

You might be asking yourself, *How will I benefit from this book if I do not have any experience in the market? Will it give me the necessary knowledge to enter the market and start my career as a developer?* I can assure you that the answer to the second question is "yes." Let me tell you more about some of the benefits that this book and learning Java will bring you.

## The Benefits

Apart from the financial benefits of learning Java, this book will bring you practical and to-the-point information that will enable you to use shortcuts that took me a long time to learn. The benefit of reading something written by someone with experience on the job means that you will get theoretical information and practical applications of Java in real life. This includes setting up your project from beginning to finish and debugging and fixing errors you might find along the way.

The information I share with you, the reader, is a result of years of working with Java in different companies with different applications. Because of its OOP, you will find an application for it almost anywhere, fitting into the concept known as WORE—write once run everywhere. This means you can apply it in mobile and cloud applications, games, and other projects.

Although I will keep the language simple throughout the book, you will see that Java is very user-friendly and easy to learn. One of the main reasons for this is that you do not need to memorize long syntaxes. The other is the wide range of libraries and tutorials that you can find online in case you have any doubt that persists—the support system in the Java community is vastly available in the market and on the internet, making it close to none.

The concepts aggregated in this book will make this a useful reference in case of any doubts or problems throughout your development process. I suggest you keep it next to you while you try out the proposed exercises and step-by-step processes so that you can refer right back to it in case you have any doubts. Keep in mind that you should always try the proposed solutions to ensure that you understand the concept—having a hands-on approach is the best way to learn! Keep a notebook beside you if you need to take notes or write down any thoughts.

**What Will Change?**

Once you finish this book, you will be able to have a vast idea about Java and programming with the language. I will provide you with all the knowledge needed to start a career and work your way up to becoming a proficient developer. You will also have a reference book to guide you and answer any questions you might have throughout your learning process. You can effortlessly create your virtual Java machine, debug problems, and efficiently code to reach your objective.

# About the Author

My name is Scott Brandt, and I am a Java developer and the author of *Java from Zero*. My work is focused on helping beginners and professionals build their understanding and skills in Java to program at a proficient level.

Throughout my career, I have been responsible for using Java to program software and applications, collaborating with engineers and web developers to ensure that solutions meet individual businesses' needs. This involves seeing products through to the end of their development from the beginning of the process. Now working at a senior level, I am involved in everything from architecture to design to implementation, but I remember vividly how daunting it was to learn the language in the early days.

Having worked with many junior-level programmers and identified the gaps in their understanding, I resolved to provide a clear-cut approach to understanding Java so fully that the journey towards becoming an expert is not only simple but a natural progression.

I am married with three young children and enjoy outdoor sports and spending time with my family. Despite my demanding career as a developer, I also love spending my free time developing my own programs and expanding my skills.

# Chapter 1: Setting Up Your Development Environment

The first thing you need to do when you want to start developing in Java, or in any other language for that matter, is to set up the environment. Although Java is a platform-independent language, its components, such as the Java Development Kit (JDK), Java Runtime Environment (JRE), and the Java Virtual Machine (JVM), depend on the platform you are going to use.

For a brief explanation, since we will see this further along, the JDK is the software that you have to download to start the development, the JRE is composed of the libraries that you will need to run the program and is considered to be "within" the JDK, and finally, the JVM is a virtual machine where the code will be executed, and it is located within the JRE sphere with other files you might have in your computer. These are all some of the tools that you will use and that will help you develop. Let's take a deeper look at some of them.

# Tools for Java Development

Before you start developing, you will need to download a few tools that will enable you to program. The three basic items are the JDK, an integrated development environment (IDE) software, and a build tool and development manager. The JDK can be downloaded from one of the several online sources, which we will see in a bit, and the IDE and build manager will depend on your preference. In this section, I will show you a bit more of them based on my personal preference and popularity, but this does not mean there aren't other places you can go to obtain them.

### The Java Development Kit

The JDK can be found online, and the version you choose will depend on the objective of your program. The "official" place to get it is on Oracle's website, which is the owner of the language and periodically updates its features. "However, other places such as Amazon, for example, have their own JDK oriented towards developing software according to their needs. You will need to remember that the JDK you download needs to be compatible with your operational system—there are versions available for Windows, macOS, Linux, and Solaris.

When you download the JDK, it will automatically bring you the "Java Runtime Environment (JRE), an interpreter/loader (Java), a compiler (javac), an archiver (JAR), a documentation generator (Javadoc) and other tools needed in Java development" (Techopedia, 2020). All of the tools that are downloaded are essential for your environment setup.

One of the most common confusions that new developers make with Java is to confuse and interchange the JDK with the JRE. The JRE comes with the JDK, enabling you to run applications, while the JDK is used for compiling programs. We could say that the JDK is the toolbox and the JRE is one of the tools that it contains. While you could use each other separately, the JDK will be essential for the developer.

However, although the JDK is essential, it does not enable you to write code within it. Therefore, unless you want to manually write your code and check endless lines of it by using a simple word editing tool, you will need a place to organize all the information and facilitate your production process. This is enabled by the next tool we will talk about, the integrated development environment.

*An Integrated Development Environment*

As you might imagine, the final objective of setting up the environment is to have a place where you can write and execute the code for your program productively. The integrated development environment (IDE) is an essential tool since it is where you will be working most of the time. It is a platform that will allow you to code more easily and efficiently— today, no programmer, independent of the language they choose to develop in, develops without an IDE.

The main reason is that its characteristics enable them to produce in a central environment where all the information will be compiled, facilitating the constantly changing screens. "IDEs typically provide a code editor, a compiler or interpreter and a debugger that and some much more the developer accesses through a unified graphical user interface" (TechTarget, 2016, para. 2). Everything you need, from a place to keep the database to a file manager, will be contained within this IDE.

Because it has all of these features, Java (and other) developers choose to integrate their IDEs into their environment preparation process. Think about it this way: When you develop, you use several screens, among which is the one where you write the code and the one where you execute it. With it, if there is a mistake in your code, it will work as an "autocorrect" and "autocomplete" by giving suggestions that will identify for the developer the place where the mistake was made without having to go over the full code again.

There are a few types of IDEs that are popular with developers, of which I have chosen to mention three out of the many lists that exist and based on my experience. They are Eclipse, the most popular, Java Visual Studio Code, and IntelliJ Idea. The choice of IDE you will use will depend on what kind of programming you will perform and the development's final objective.

These platforms mostly provide the same services, although some versions of IDEs are paid, and others offer a free version—it will depend on your needs. To sum it up, your experience, skills, and team process will determine your choice—ultimately, your preference will impact the decision the most.

### Build Tool and Dependency Manager

When you have several libraries you want to work from, it might be hard to manage all the information you wish to compile. Libraries are essential for the work of a developer. Although it is possible to develop without them, it is unlikely this would be a wise use of your time since it would take longer and make productivity decline. When you have a dependency manager, you will use it to manage all the libraries that will facilitate the coding process and keep track of what you are doing and need.

To manage all this information, you should use what developers call a build tool and dependency manager, or a package manager. "This is a program or command-line utility that automates the process of compiling, assembling, and deploying software" (Devopscube, 2022), speeding up your production and making it easier to manage the dependencies and the dependencies within the dependencies, as well as help you with integration. In simple words, you will be able to target the specific items you need for a determined project that will use a specific language.

Suppose you have a project and are unsure of the version of Java used by the library you want to apply. Or, that you want to use several libraries with a different version from the one you will be using. The dependency tool will help you find the correct library you should use by describing it to the software, and it will find it for you, making the search easier and less timely. It will also guarantee that all those working with you on the project are using the same language version, avoiding further complications and misunderstanding when it is time to integrate all the developed code into one program.

Apache Maven and Gradle are the two most popular build tools and dependency managers. Although they are similar tools, Maven is more scalable and extensible and is used by smaller teams and those who do not have the budget for more investment in the project. Some of the advantages of Maven include a specific integrated environment and that it can be installed into the machine used for coding. Maven will give the developer a place to write their code and facilitate the integration between code lines written by different people.

On the other hand, you have Gradle, considered one of the most modern build tools developed to extract from the largest variety of libraries the information that a developer will need—including information from the Maven central repository. One of the greatest advantages of Gradle is that it will help you separate what is for testing and what is for the actual production environment. It is also helpful that Gradle will allow you to debug your code if there is a problem with the version of the library you are using, enabling the quick and easy update of the new information to fix the problem.

To compare both tools, we could say that "Gradle resolves dependency conflicts differently than Maven, usually finding the latest version of the dependency rather than simply choosing the dependency closest to the project in the dependency tree" (Xu, 2022, Gradle section, para. 4). As I mentioned earlier, the other kit tools will all depend on your personal preference and the tools the teams are using. There are other package managers you could use; exploring them will help you make a better decision. In any case, independent of the one you select, it is important to have one and integrate it with your development environment.

**Setting Up Your Development Environment**

Now that you know the basic items you will need to set up your environment, it is time to make it happen. For this book, I will use installation and configuration examples for devices that use the Windows operating system. It is important to remember that each item you will use needs to be compatible with the system to avoid mistakes or problems when it is time to execute the code. I will also use the most common and official sources of information for this general purpose, although it is perfectly fine if you decide to use another choice based on the project you are working on. Are you ready?

*Installing the JDK*

The first thing you need to do is go to the Oracle website and download the JDK. Here, you must pay attention to the operating system since it provides download options for Linux, macOS, and, lastly, Windows. Click on the link for the appropriate version, and a window will be opened asking where you want to save the file. Remember to note where it is being saved since you will need to access it later in the following steps.

Next, you will have two options to open the environment variables. The first is to follow the path: **Control Panel > System and Security > System**. You will select the "Environment Variables" option under the "Advanced" system setting. The other way to do this is to go to your start menu in the taskbar and type "edit environment variables for your account." The option should appear once you are done typing the first few words. Once it does, click on it to open.

Once you have done this, both options will take you to the same screen, where you can edit the variables for your computer. A list of the system variables will appear, and you will have two possibilities. The first is that the JDK appears in the list. If this happens, you should select the one that refers to the path where it is and click on "Edit." A new window will open where you will have the variable name and the variable value. You will make the following changes in the value: adding a semicolon to the end and adding the installation location with **\bin** after it. Once the path has been created, click on "Ok" to finalize the process.

On the other hand, if the path does not appear for you, you will need to create it. To do this, you should click on the "New" button after the system variables list. Once the window opens, you will add to the "Value" field the path where the JDK is located (remember, you took note of it?). The path should match the exact place where the files are located. Once you are done, save the setting and, just as in the other process, click on "Ok" to finalize. Your JDK is now installed, but it is wise to conduct a small test to ensure it.

To conduct the test, go to the taskbar and type in *cmd* to open the command prompt. Once the window opens, you should type in *java -version* (the word java, a space, a dash, and the word version) and hit enter. If it responds to you by bringing the Java version, you have successfully installed the JDK. However, if the message you read says "Not recognized," you should go back to the previous steps and see if you have made a mistake or missed something throughout the process. Once you have confirmed that the JDK is installed, you are now ready to set up the IDE.

*Installing the IDE*

For the IDE, I have chosen to use Eclipse because of its popularity and features. It is important to note that you will only be able to download the software if you already have the JDK installed on your machine since this is a prerequisite. Once you have done this, you should go to the Eclipse website to download it. There, you will find what is called an Eclipse Installer, which is a tool that will help you with the process.

The first thing you should do, as you might imagine, is to download the installer to your computer. Here, you should note that just as with the JDK, there are versions of Eclipse for macOS, Windows, and Linux, and you should choose the one that matches the operational system you are using. When downloading in Windows, once the process is complete, a new window will open asking if you want to execute the .exe file for the software. Here, note that the publisher should be Eclipse Foundation, Inc.

Once you open the file, you will select the Eclipse IDE for Java developers and save the file on your computer. You can choose the place you want to save, and I suggest doing it with all the files you will use for the project. Next, click on "Install." Once this is done, you can launch the program and start configuring it.

One essential thing in this process is to be aware and sure of your configuration choices. The reason for this is that this will hugely impact your development—for good or bad. If the configuration process is done well, you will see your process flow effortlessly and without many problems. However, if you make any mistakes during the configuration, this may lead to future problems and bugs that will take up your time during the development. But do not worry if you have no idea how to do this! In the next chapter, we will go through all the steps necessary to configure Eclipse correctly so that you avoid any potential problems during the creation of your project.

## *Installing Build Tool and Dependency Manager*

Now that you have both the JDK and the IDE ready and installed, it is time to select the build tool you will use. I have chosen to use Apache Maven because of its integration with Eclipse and the IDE's support for this tool. Your preference will play a large role in this selection, and although it is not mandatory to have a build tool, I would highly recommend it because it will make your life easier.

As commonly known in the market, Maven does not have distinct versions based on the operating system; it is one version for all. However, it does require that you have the JDK installed on your computer as a prerequisite. You must go to the Apache official website and click the download button to download the software. Once you have done this, a file will be available on your computer with a .zip extension that you will need to extract.

Now, remember the process you had to follow to install the JDK on your computer? You will do the same thing to install Maven. Go to "Environment Variables" in the settings and, in the advanced tab, select the environment variable button. Here, it is generally unlikely that it will be already installed, so you will need to create a variable name, usually "Maven_Home," and paste the path in the variable value line—it should be the place where the file is located. Add the \bin extension to the variable's name by using "Edit" and then "New" in the edit environment variable. Once you have done this, Maven will be installed.

You can run a test in your computer's command prompt to ensure everything went as expected. Type in *cmd* in the navigation pane to find the application and open it. Once the window appears, you will type *mvn -version* (the letters "mvn," space, dash, and the word "version"). This should make the information that Apache Maven has been installed and is ready to be used. In case you see information that is not recognized, you should go back and trace all your steps to see if you did not make any mistakes. You now have all the tools you need to start your first project!

## Summary

In this chapter, you have seen how to set up the basic tools for developing in Java.

The first and essential step you will need to take is downloading the JDK since it will be a prerequisite for installing the IDE and the build manager.

I have taken you through the process step by step, and you now have all the tools you will need to start working on your first Java project.

In the next chapter, you will see how to configure the tools you have downloaded and how to start your new project from scratch.

# Chapter 2: Setting Up Your Own Java Project

At first, the idea of setting up your own Java project may seem intimidating. But it's, as you will see, this is something that is not difficult to do. Anyone can set up a project and start writing code with the right tools and a little knowledge.

**How to Set Up Your Own Java Project**

Once you have your environment set up and all the requisites for your program prepared, it is time to start. Since we will be working with the Eclipse IDE rather than a simple text tool, you will need to open the software to start your project. To do this, double-click on the icon for Eclipse, select **New**, and then **Create a Java Project**. As an alternative to following the paths and clicking, you can use the shortcut **Alt + Shift + N**, which will open a new project.

*Creating a Project*

To create a new project, you should follow the above path, which will lead you to a new window asking you to write down the project name. Type in the name of your project, for example, *MyFirstJavaProject*. You can determine a default location where the project will be saved or set another destination according to your preference. Next, select the version of Java you want to use based on the specification of your client or your organization. This will be done in the window section under JRE, which you have already installed as part of the JDK.

**Pro tip**: Here, ensure that the version of the JDK is the same as the version you want to work in. If not, you will need to install the version in Preferences and then Install **JREs**. These options are available in the **Configure JREs**... link in this section. You will also check if the versions are the same here.

Once you have done this, a new window will open with the name of your project and a folder with the letters **src** under them. Do not change any of the configurations on this page for now, and click on **Finish** for the project to open on your workspace. Congratulations! You have finished setting up your template and begun your first Java project! Pat yourself on the back if you tried this on your computer, and it worked. If it didn't, don't worry—go back and read the first chapter and the beginning of this chapter again to see if you didn't miss anything.

**Pro tip**: Once the project is available in your workspace, it is important to guarantee that the folder **JRE System Library** shows as a subfolder. This is because it refers to the Java library that will be used for your project, without which you do not have Java support and, therefore, cannot create a new one.

Now, all that is left is a few minor setups and finally, start writing your code! However, let's not get ahead of ourselves. Before we effectively *write* the code, I'd say it would be important to understand *how* to write it. Therefore, we will take a moment to learn a little about Java syntax and some of its basic features. Don't worry if these seem generic at first. In the next chapter, we will put all of the information you have learned here to use and will be able to see how to put them into practice.

## Writing Code in Java

Before we start writing code in Java, you will need to know a few rules that apply to the coding. This mainly happens because each language has rules and definitions that will enable the developer to create its program. These include how to make comments, what classes and objects are, and other basic items that must be considered while developing. Remember that these are just a small introduction to each; we will see more of them throughout the book, with examples. Let's take a look at them.

- **Object**: An object is also known as an instance in Java. These will hold their characteristics, such as states and behaviors. Think about a lion, for example. It has its physical characteristics and behavioral traits. Therefore, in this case, your object would be the lion. When you have an object, it is identified by three different features: identity, state, and behavior. Identity will be what makes it unique, state describes what individual characteristics this object has, and behavior refers to what the object does.

- **Class**: We now know what an object is, making it easier to understand a class. A class is a blueprint or a set of objects with the same characteristics and properties. Although they will group the information, the class is not something that is in the real world, they are something that will allow the object to be created; we could say that it is a prototype. In a class, there will be a group of variables with different information and method groups. If you think about a house, for example, its blueprint will be similar to what a class is for Java.

- **Method**: The method is equivalent to the behavior of the object. Because of its characteristics, a class can, for example, have several methods or behaviors. It is here that the action and the logic will be written. Based on what is written here, you will execute the command you have determined and manipulate the data you wish to manage. Essentially, the method will be the code you will write that will conduct the action that the code contains.

- **Expression**: An expression in Java is the part of the code that consists of variables, methods, and operators. The expression will be created according to the language syntax. An expression is the core component of a statement.

- **Statements**: A statement in Java is equivalent to a sentence in a normal language (Oracle, n.d.-b. However, the developer will use a semicolon ";" instead of a period to end the statement.

**Pro tip**: Java has a list of words considered "reserved." This means that they cannot be used throughout your coding because they already have a specific use within the language. To avoid problems while coding, every Java developer should memorize these words—it will be an essential part of your learning process.

Here is a list of these 50 words:

| abstract | continue | for | new | switch |
| assert | default | goto | package | synchronized |
| boolean | do | if | private | this |
| break | double | implements | protected | throw |
| byte | else | import | public | throws |
| case | enum | instanceof | return | transient |
| catch | extends | int | short | try |
| char | final | interface | static | void |
| class | finally | long | strictfp | volatile |
| const | float | native | super | while |

## *Running Your Project*

While compiling and running your code will be simple if you are using an IDE, I would like to teach you how to do this when using a simple text editor such as the built-in Notepad app. Although most developers will use the IDE and just click on a button to make things work, you need to know how to do this if the IDE is unavailable.

Therefore, suppose that you are writing your code in the Notepad or TextEdit applications on your computer for this section. You will use this and the command prompt to compile and run your newly-developed Java code. It is important to remember that although you will not be using an IDE, the JDK still needs to be installed on your computer as a prerequisite.

### Compiling the Code

Once you are done typing your code in the text editor, you will need to save the file. Now, let's suppose that you want to name your file *MyFirstJavaProject*. You will need to save it on your computer as *MyFirstJavaProject.java.* To compile the program, you should open the command prompt (cmd) on your computer; once the screen opens, type in the following: javac MyFirstJavaProgram.java and then hit enter. This should compile your code and make it ready to run.

**Pro tip**: When you try to compile your code, you might receive an error message saying that **javac is not recognized as an internal or external command, operable program, or batch file**. This means that your computer does not recognize the path it needs to compile the program, and thus, you will need to establish a path for it in your computer. To do this, in the same command application in your Windows, "go to the place where you have installed Java on your system and locate the bin directory, copy the complete path and write it in the command like this: set path=C:\Program Files\Java\jdk1.8.0_121\bin" (Singh, 2013a). Here, you must remember to adapt this line according to the Java and JDK versions that you have on your computer.

### Running the Code

Once you have compiled your code and the information is set, you will be able to run your code. To do this, still in the command menu, type in java MyFirstJavaProgram and press Enter. Once you have done this, the result will be available on the window (Tutorials Point, n.d.-c).

*Debugging Your Project*

Nothing will be more frustrating for you as the developer if you have code that does not work. While it will be simple to find the mistakes when you have written a short code, dealing with lines and more lines of text will be more challenging. And this is exactly where having an IDE installed on your computer will prove fruitful.

Instead of spending hours trying to identify where and what you did wrong, you will be able to find the answers by clicking on a button, or it will show you the mistake you made while typing. Since we installed the Eclipse IDE in the beginning on your computer, this will be the standard that I will use to explain how to fix errors in your code.

You will first need to run the code completely to see if any mistakes can be found. Once this is done, you must consider the places in the syntax where the mistakes are highlighted. If you have used a compiler for your code, this will make it easier to find the mistakes once you run the code. The error message will appear on your screen once you run the program. In the IDE, you will see a separate tab where you will find all the errors it found while running the program (Nehra, 2022). In Eclipse, the debugging button will be the one with the image of a "bug" (as in insect) on it.

When using Eclipse, the first thing you need to do is to use the package explorer view. First, right-click on the class that contains the main method, and under **Debug As**, select the second option, **Java application**. One of the shortcuts you can use is tapping the **Alt + Shift + D** and **J** on your keyboard. This will enable you to set up the configurations for your debugging. However, if your option is to directly debug the code, then all you need to do is to press **F11**.

**Pro tip**: One of the things that you will be able to do when writing your code in Eclipse is to set breakpoints that will enable you to "mark" your program and make it easier to find the mistake. When you add a breakpoint, this means that when you run the debugger, it will stop once it reaches this marker. This will allow your code to be broken down into several sections, making it easier to identify where the mistake is located instead of looking at the full code at once. "To set a breakpoint, in the editor area right, click on the marker bar and select Toggle Breakpoint" (Tutorials Point, n.d.-d, para. 7) or use the shortcut **Ctrl + Shift + B**. You should apply this step before going into production with your code.

If you still have doubts regarding the process, do not worry. We will dive deeper into the subject of debugging further ahead in Chapter 14.

## Distributing Your Project

Once you are done with your code and have compiled and run it, it is time to "publish" or distribute it. This means you will be delivering your program to the final user, and they will be able to use it. "The methods used by developers to build, test and deploy new code will impact how fast a product can respond to changes in customer preferences or requirements and the quality of each change" (Every Answer, 2022, What is the meaning of deploy in programming section). An easy way to think about it is to imagine an army. When they say that the battalion has been *deployed*, they have been put in place to start the action.

As we will see more on how to distribute your Java program in Chapter 17, in this section, I will just go over the basic idea of the process. You will first need to save the file into a Java archive (JAR) file and sign it. When you compile something into JAR, you are compressing it so that it occupies less space possible in your computer's memory.

If you are using the Java Web Start applications, you will need to use the Java Network Launch Protocol (JNLP), a file you will need to deploy the program. You can use deployment whether you are using an IDE or not. This will depend on the user preference and the method you have chosen to write your code.

Once you have a JNLP file, you can run your code from a web browser. All you will need to do if your program was written in Notepad and with the name of the project we have previously used is type in the browser address field: `<a href="/some/path/MyFirstJavaProgram.jnlp">Launch Notepad Application</a>` (Oracle, n.d.-b). Other options for deploying your program include running it through your computer's cache or the desktop.

If you choose the first option, you can run the Java Start Web application in the Java Cache Viewer, and the application will be listed for you to select and run it. To do this, click on a button similar to a "pay" button or double-click on the intended program. If your choice is to run it on your desktop, you must create a shortcut to the program and select it as you would with any other application. If these concepts seem vague to you, don't worry. We will see more of it a little bit ahead.

# Summary

In this chapter, you have learned some of the steps you will need to perform, from starting to write your Java program to deploying it.

Although it might have seemed that we just skimmed through the concepts, rest assured that we will go over them again in further detail in the coming chapters.

One of the main things you should remember from this chapter are the 50 keywords that cannot be used while you are coding.

This will prove to be especially useful starting in the next chapter when we will go over creating your first Java program.

# Chapter 3: Creating Your First Java Program

I bet you are already excited to start your first Java program, am I right? So without further delay, let's take a look at the basics of creating a Java project, adding classes, and running multiple programs when using an IDE. In this chapter, you will learn to create and run your own Java project from start to finish.

Although many details entail creating a Java project, you have already done one of the main parts, which is setting up the environment. Since you will be using the IDE to write your code, we will build your skills by giving you the step-by-step process to start your program based on Eclipse.

Now, if you have followed this read and completed the same processes on your computer, this will be easier to follow. Therefore, I recommend that if you haven't done so, you go back and set up everything so you can conduct the steps as we walk through them.

Remember back in Chapter 2 when we created our first project named *MyFirstJavaProject*? If you don't take a moment, look back at the information I provided to refresh your memory. Since the project was already created at that instance, we will now move on to adding classes and other actions you will need to perform to make your program work before effectively writing the code itself.

**Adding a Package**

Now that you have created the project, you will see a tab to the left of your screen that says **Package Explorer**. In there, you should see your project *MyFirstJavaProject* written next to a folder and under it, another one that is written *src* and then JRE System Library. The next step is to create a package to help you organize your project and the directories you choose.

To create a package, right-click on the name of the project, prompting a drop-down menu to open. In it, you should click on **New** and then on the next window on **Package**. A dialogue box will open where you should add the name of your package. The package's name will depend on the company policy, but in general, it will be similar to an internet address structure in large organizations with several subdivisions.

In this case, let's suppose that the name we will create for the package will be com.mycompany.projectone. Click on finish, and your package has been installed. To confirm you have correctly created a package, look at the package explorer folder and see if the file with the name you typed appears there.

**Java convention**: One of the first Java conventions you should know to make the code easier for you and other developers to understand is how to name a package. In this case, the convention says that the name you choose for the package should be all in lowercase and that their names should have a meaning that others will understand.

**Adding a Main Class**

After creating a package, it is time to create a class, which will enable you to write your code. A class is known to developers as a "factory" or template to create objects. The process will be similar to creating a package. You will right-click on the package in the file explorer tab, and a menu will open. There, you should select **New** and then **Class**. Next to the field where it says **Name**, you will write the name you wish to add to your project. In this case, I will use *MyFirstClass*.

**Java convention**: When naming a class, ensure that the first letter of each word is capitalized and that there are no spaces between the words. Since your program will generally use something real, try incorporating the term into your name so it is easier to be identified. In our case, we have capitalized the M, the F, and the C in *MyFirstClass*.

In the next section, where you are asked which modifier you want, maintain the "public" box checked. Do not make any other changes to the settings, but ensure that the **public**

**static void main(String[] args)** box under method stubs is checked for your first projects. Once you are done, click on finish.

Now, if you look at the package explorer folder, you will see that under the package icon appears the class that you have just created. On the screen to the right, the following should show:

package com.mycompany.projectone;

public class MyFirstClass {

public static void main (String[] args) {

// TODO Auto-generated method stub

}

}

## Writing Your First Java Program

You have successfully created your package and your class, and, therefore, all that is left is the coding of your first program. To do this, we will ask the program to print out the words "Hello World," which is pretty much a standard for beginner developers. At the end of the code you saw previously, you will type in System.out.println("Hello World!"). On your Java editor, it should look like this:

```java
package com.mycompany.projectone;

public class MyFirstClass {

public static void main (String[] args) {

System.out.println("Hello World!");

}

}
```

## Running Your Code

It is now time to run your code. To do this, you have two options: the first is to right-click on the class name in the project and then click on **Run As**. The other option is to go to the top navigation bar, select **Run,** and afterward, **Run As** and select your program name. A shortcut for this using your keyboard would be by tapping **Alt + Shift + X**, and **J**. Once you have commanded your program to run, a tab will appear at the bottom of the screen with the word **Console** written on it. This is where you will see the result of your code line, in this case, the words *Hello World*. And that's it! You have successfully created your first Java project!

**Pro tip**: One of the advantages of using the IDE is that it will automatically compile your code for you, making it needless to do so manually. Additionally, if there is a problem in the code, a tab at the bottom of your screen will immediately appear with the word **Problems** on it. You can click on it, and it will indicate the problem and the location (line) where the problem is located.

**Adding a Second Class**

If you want to add a second class to your program, you will need to follow the same steps you did for creating the first class. In the **src** folder, right-click and select **new** and then **class**. Once you have done this, give your second class another name according to the convention you previously read about. Suppose the name you created for the second class is *SecondClass*. In this case, a new tab will open at the top of your Java editor with the name "Second Class."

It should appear as the following:

package com.mycompany.projectone;

public class Second Class {

public static void main (String[] args) {

// TODO Auto-generated method stub

}

}

**Pro tip**: You cannot create two main methods in the same Java class. If you do this, the compiler will return an error to you. Therefore, the solution is to either remove the public declaration from one of them by unclicking on the **public static void main(String args)** box when creating the class, rename the file with a .java extension, or separate the classes.

Therefore, when you see your code, you will need to use one of the options above to change it to:

public class SecondClass {

}

Most developers use multiple classes in their programs so that they do not need to code in different windows and compile different parts of the code. However, you must remember that although you can create as many classes as you want, this is not recommended if you are just starting since you can get lost in all the lines of code you will have. It also makes the code harder to read and interpret for other developers. One of the options here is to create a single file for each of the classes that you want to use in your program.

**Running Multiple Programs**

If your option is to run multiple programs at the same time, this is also possible using Eclipse. The first thing you will need to do you have already done: creating a new class under the **Main** class. Based on the previous steps, suppose you have two tabs on your Java editor. The first is the "Hello World" we wrote in the first place.

package com.mycompany.projectone;

public class MyFirstClass {

public static void main (String[] args) {

System.out.println("Hello World!");

}

}

The second will be based on the second class that we created that should print out *How are you?*

```java
public class SecondClass {

System.out.println ("How are you?");

}
```

To run both programs, you will need two consoles. After you have created the new console, you will need to run the first code. Once you run it, if you click on either console, you will see that they are both running the program. To solve this, you will click on the button that "pins" the program to the chosen console. Next, run the second code the same way. Nothing will change in the console where you pinned the first program, but on the second console, you will see that the other program is running. Both programs are now running simultaneously. Pin the second program to the second console accordingly.

**Pro tip**: To see both programs running simultaneously on the same screen, move each console to a separate view. This will enable you to see each of them working and give you a general view of what is happening in both instances.

## Summary

You must be excited that you have just finished writing your first code. Way to go! If there are any error mistakes once you run them, be sure to go back and see if you did not make any mistakes.

Remember that Eclipse will give you the line where the problem is; therefore, it should be easy to identify what you did wrong.

I recommend you try some other codes based on what you have learned in this section to practice your skills. Once you are done, move on to the next chapter.

There, I will teach you all about using comments in your Java code and how to use them.

# Chapter 4: Using Comments in Java

When developers write their code, they might resort to the alternative of making comments within its lines to make it easier to understand what they meant by such code. In this chapter, I will explain to you how you can use comments so that the information is not compiled by the builder and that you can make any observations you deem necessary. We will see what comments are, how to write them in Java, and tips to write them effectively. You will also learn how to automate documentation creation by using comments within the code lines.

Suppose you are working on a project with other developers and each of you has a part of the program you are in charge of. Like handwriting or a way of speaking, each coder has their own way of writing code and their signature. For this reason, if you are working with more than one person, you might have different characteristics and the others might not understand what you mean. In this case, if you want to make yourself clear or understand what a colleague has written, you will need to use comments, which will prove themselves to be very helpful.

## What Are Comments?

You might have felt a little confused when I mentioned that you would write your comments within your code. But you did read it right. There are methods used to comment on what has been written and make it not be executed by the program. One of the advantages of using comments is that it will enable you to understand exactly what the developer meant by writing that line of code, and it will make it easier for you to find problems and debug the program. You can use the comments to explain anything within the code—from the variable to any statement.

# How to Write Comments in Java

To understand writing comments in Java, you first need to understand that there are three types you can use:

1. Single-line comments
2. Multi-line comments
3. Documentation comments

Each of these will serve a different purpose and have a different methodology to apply. Let's take a look at what each of these is and how to use them.

**Single-Line Comments**

Single-line comments are the most common and usually found with code, especially if they are done by newbies. The syntax for these types of comments is the easiest: You will add a double forward slash to the beginning of the line or the end of the code and write what you want to write. For example:

```
//This will be your comment
```

In our code from the previous chapter, it would look something like this:

```
package com.mycompany.projectone;

public class MyFirstClass {

public static void main (String[] args) {

//I want to print a greeting when the program starts

System.out.println("Hello World!");
```

}

}

In this case, you are explaining to the other developers who will read the code that your intention with this line of code is to print a greeting. However, the output of the program when you run it will still be *Hello World!* This is because anything that was written after the slashes until the end of the line will be ignored by the compiler, and your outcome will still be the same.

Another thing you can do is add the comment to the end of the code. By using the same example as before, if you add it to the end, it would look like this:

package com.mycompany.projectone;

public class MyFirstClass {

public static void main (String[] args) {

System.out.println("Hello World!"); //I want to print a greeting when the program starts

}

}

## *Multi-Line Comments*

Multi-line comments are used when there is the need to explain more complex code— you can use it to comment on a part of the multiple lines of the code you are working on. Because using the double forward slash (//) for every single line can become somewhat laborious, developers choose the multi-line approach when the explanation is extensive. These comments will also be placed within the lines of code but written between /* and */. For example:

/*

Use multi-line comments

such as this one

when you are

using more extensive

explanations

*/

Once again, we will apply this to our previous code. It would look like this:

In this case, the output will still be *Hello World.*

**Pro tip**: You can also use the formatting of the multi-line code for single-lined comments. In this case, you will apply the same logic, but the /* and the */ will be in the same line. For example, /*This is my comment*/.

### Documentation Comments

If you are creating a large program such as software or a project that will require many lines of code, you can use the documentation comments feature to help generate the supporting files for the program—it will enable you to register the methods and the method signature of the program. These will be used as references for others regarding the product's parameters and methods. To create your documentation while writing your code, you will need to use the **Javadoc tool**. It will help you create an API that will generate the documentation for everything that is between the /** and the */ symbols.

You will notice that in this instance, there are two asterisks instead of one. This is because when you are commenting in Javadoc, comments need to start with a forward dash and two asterisks, different from the multi-line comments where only one is used.

**Pro tip**: To generate the Javadoc tool in your Eclipse, you will need to follow a few steps. This is what you should do, according to Minh (2019): Once in the IDE, select **Generate Javadoc** in the project menu for the wizard of the tool to appear. In the window, you will need to select the location of the program on your computer, which is generally in the JAVA_HOME bin directory.

Next, you should use the same feature to identify the project for which you want to use the tool and what kinds of Javadocs you want to generate. Here, it is important to select them carefully because all of them are already checked by default. Next, limit the class and choose the visibility so that you know what will be printed. Finally, specify the destination where the generated documentation should be saved and click on **Next**.

In the next screens, you will be able to specify the characteristics of the documents. Keep in mind to check the *Open generated index file in browser* to generate the document in Eclipse's internal browser and to click on *Save the setting of this Javadoc export as an Ant script* so that it automatically generates the documents as the projects develop.

**Using Tags**

One of the things you will be able to use when generating document comments is a tool known as a tag. These will tell the program what exactly it is you want to generate. A few tags can be used, and while some are more common than others, they will make your document generation faster and easier to understand. Below you will find a table with the links extracted from Agarwal (2017, C. Documentation Comments section):

| Tag | Description | Syntax |
| --- | --- | --- |
| @author | Adds the author of a class. | @author name-text |
| {@code} | Displays text in code font without interpreting the text as HTML markup or nested Javadoc tags. | {@code text} |

| {@docRoot} | Represents the relative path to the generated document's root directory from any generated page. | {@docRoot} |
|---|---|---|
| @deprecated | Adds a comment indicating that this API should no longer be used. | @deprecated deprecatedtext |
| @exception | Adds a Throws subheading to the generated documentation, with the class name and description text. | @exception class-name description |
| {@inheritDoc} | Inherits a comment from the nearest inheritable class or implementable interface. | Inherits a comment from the immediate superclass. |
| {@link} | Inserts an in-line link with the visible text label that points to the documentation for the specified package, class, or member name of a referenced class. | {@link package.class#member label} |
| {@linkplain} | Identical to {@link}, except the link's label is displayed in plain text rather than code font. | {@linkplain package.class#member label} |

| | | |
|---|---|---|
| @param | Adds a parameter with the specified parameter name followed by the specified description to the "Parameters" section. | @param parameter-name description |
| @return | Adds a "Returns" section with the description text. | @return description |
| @see | Adds a "See Also" heading with a link or text entry that points to reference. | @see reference |
| @serial | Used in the doc comment for a default serializable field. | @serial field-description \| include \| exclude |
| @serialData | Documents the data written by the writeObject( ) or writeExternal( ) methods. | @serialData data-description |
| @serialField | Documents an ObjectStreamField component. | @serialField field-name field-type field-description |
| @since | Adds a "Since" heading with the specified since-text to the generated documentation. | @since release |

| @throws | The @throws and @exception tags are synonyms. | @throws class-name description |
| --- | --- | --- |
| {@value} | When {@value} is used in the doc comment of a static field, it displays the value of that constant. | {@value package.class#field} |
| @version | Adds a "Version" subheading with the specified version text to the generated docs when the -version option is used. | @version version-text |

This is what your code would look like this with document comments:

```
package com.mycompany.projectone;
/**
*Greeting the user when the program opens
*@author Scott Brandt
*@since 2022-01-01
*@version 2.0
*/
public class MyFirstClass {
/**
*This program will be user-friendly and should greet the user once they log in.
*@see More information
*/
public static void main (String[] args) {
```

```
System.out.println("Hello World!");
    }
}
```

# Using Comments

If you are new to the Java world, you are probably unaware that using comments is somewhat of a major discussion between developers. While some people believe and defend that comments should not be written because the code should be self-explanatory, others say that comments are essential if they want others to understand what was done. In addition to this, those who are against using comments within the code claim that too much time is wasted when comments are being written and that they create "noise" where there is supposed to be none.

Although I will not enter this discussion because it will not effectively add to the knowledge that you are acquiring, I will go over some of the reasons why you should use comments, how not to use them, and some of the conventions that should be applied if you do decide to use them. After you have this section, it will be up to you whether to use them or not.

### *Why Use Comments?*

If you are in doubt about using comments or not, consider the following list. Comments can:

- make the code easier to read and understand.

- help you experiment with different codes and ways to improve them by adding a "reminder" of sorts.

- explain the reasons for a specific line of code, such as a business decision.

- aid you in remembering what the code does if you return to it after not looking at it for a while.

- write out the strategy that you will use without having to focus on the code itself—think about it as writing an explanation that will allow you to see the rationale that you want to apply.

- be useful for debugging purposes by temporarily removing parts of the code to see if that fixes the problem.

- help in generating documentation.

- create warnings or alert signs regarding the code and what will happen if it is modified.

- explain your code and reasoning to less experienced developers as a training method.

## *How NOT to Use Comments*

If you choose to use comments, keep in mind a few pointers on how they should not be used to avoid creating conflict with more senior developers. Don't write comments that:

- are longer than a couple of lines. If you need to write a lengthy explanation, it is probably a sign that the code is not well-written and could be improved.

- state the obvious or duplicate the code.

- are redundant when the code already tells us what is happening.

- will make it more confusing for others to understand what you have tried to do. If you don't understand it, it is likely others won't as well.

- justify using long syntaxes or more than one function in the same line—doing this is bad since each function should have its own line.

- have their main objective as disguising bad code or unclear statements. You should instead try to clean up the code and make it understandable.

- can change in content and meaning if the code is modified.

- have their main objective as embellishing the code, such as titles and headings for the lines of code that are to come.

- come embedded with a TO DO option. You should not write what should be done but rather just do it already since it is unlikely you will come back just to erase this piece of information from your code, especially if there are many lines to look over.

## *Tips for Using Comments Effectively*

Here are 10 best practices to rely on if you decide to use comments within your code:

1. Comments should be used to make the code easier to understand and not to state the obvious or write lengthy explanations.

2. Ensure that the comment is really necessary and that the explanation cannot be described within the code in the function or variable names.

3. Be consistent with your commenting style—if you start writing single-line comments, don't switch to multi-line comments later on. Choose one style and stick to it.

4. Respect documentation comments.

5. Don't overdo it—a few well-placed comments are better than commenting on every single line of code.

6. When fixing bugs and other problems you identify in the program during the testing phase, it is acceptable to use comments to understand and make remarks regarding what you found.

7. Use comments to cite the source of a problem or information that you are obtaining the solution from, especially external references.

8. If you are using a code you copied from somewhere else, use a comment to state the source of where you got it from.

9. Before adding a block comment to your code, use a line before and after it to separate it from the rest of the code.

10. Do not use comments as subtitles to what you intended to write.

# Exercise

Now that you know all about commenting, I want you to take a moment and go to the code you created in your IDE.

Next, try adding comments to the existing code and see if there are any mistakes. You should try applying single-line, multi-line, and documentation comments to ensure that you have understood the concepts and are able to write them without interfering with the code you have written.

Experiment as much as you like until you feel sure that you have grasped the concept. If you identify any mistakes or problems, go back and re-read the chapter to see if there are any clarifications needed.

# Summary

You now know how to create comments on your Java code. If you decide to use them, I strongly suggest that you follow the best practices outlined in the last section of this chapter.

Using them will ultimately be up to you and the team you are working with, or maybe even corporate standards.

Remember that if you start with single or multi-line comments, use them throughout the whole project so that there are no interpretation mistakes.

Ensure that the comment is really needed, and use the tips and tags I have given you to create automated documentation—this will certainly make your life easier.

You are now ready to dive deeper into Java's details and specific characteristics. The first stop is understanding and working with variables and data types.

# Chapter 5: Working With Variables and Data Types in Java

Variables and data types are two concepts essential for the Java developer to know. In spite of their importance, some people do not understand them, which can lead to problems within the code they are developing.

In this chapter, you will learn what they are and the basic concepts of working with variables and data types in Java.

You will also see how to declare and use them in expressions, when to use each one, and their applications.

## What Are Variables and Data Types?

In Java, a variable is a basic requirement because it will be the "container" of the data values that you are using. Essentially, the variable in a line of code with Java is the memory location that describes the program's unit storage. Because all programs use a certain amount of memory, you will need to declare variables before you use them. The variable will be composed of **types** and a **name**. Data is what will be stored in the in-memory variable—it is a kind of "address" to access this value in the program and the computer's memory.

To understand what is a data type in Java, first, you need to understand what are **statically** and **dynamically typed languages**. Java is a **statically typed language** where "Each variable and expression type is already known at compile time" (Agrawal, 2016, para. 1). This means that once you have dedicated a certain variable to a data type, it cannot have any other. This is the same case for other languages such as Scala, Rust, C, and C++.

On the other hand, when you have a **dynamically typed language**, such as Javascript, Python, and Ruby, the data types can be received at any moment throughout the programming, known as runtime. This means that even if the variable is assigned to the data type, there is the possibility to assign other distinct data types to the same variable throughout the programming process.

To use a variable, you need to **declare** or create it. This means giving it a name and identifying its type. To use a simple example:

You have the variable **int**. You need to give it a name; let's say it will be "day," because you want to state, for whatever reason, the day on your program. Next, you will need to assign it a value. In this case, we will say that the value will be "16." This example shows that the variable **int** has the name "day" and has the value of "16." You can write these in two ways:

int day: *(variable) → Type*

day = 16; *→ value*

or

int day = 16;

Let's use another example. In Java, if you say that the variable with the name "firstName" will have the value "Scott," it will remain as Scott within the scope (which we will learn about later) in which it was declared unless you explicitly change the value assigned to that variable. If you do not change the scope, every time you request the program to give you back the variable value, the answer will be "Scott." To change the value of the variable to "Steve," you will need to assign a new value for it. Let's take a look at an example. Your code would say:

String firstName = "Scott";

System.out.println(firstName);

"String" is the type of the variable, "firstName" is its name or characteristic, and "Scott" is the value that we want to assign to the memory.

The output, once you run the code asking for the firstName, will always be Scott because the value has not changed.

You have just assigned the word "Scott" a space in the program's memory. Let's take a look again at the first example:

int day = 16;

System.out.println(day);

Here, as we have seen, "int" is the type of the variable, "day" is the variable name, and "16" is the value that will be assigned to memory. Therefore, when you ask the program to print the "day", 16 will be the output.

Now, as I explained earlier, the variable name will not change, but you can change its value. Therefore, in the code:

String firstName = "Scott";

System.out.println(firstName); //output: Scott

firstName = "Steve";

System.out.println(firstName); //output: Steve

In this case, you have maintained that what you are doing is establishing a "String" with the name "firstName," but that the value has changed from "Scott" to "Steve" as you have seen in the comments that were made in the code above. While this might not seem as important right now, in large code bases, methods are created by others who expect specific data because of the implemented behavior, especially if you are looking at a strong data type. Many of the mistakes that appear in the runtime are reduced because when it comes time to compile the code, they will appear as a compilation error.

If you are confused by the use of "string" and "int," don't be! We will address these data types further along in the chapter, and you will be able to better understand them. Chapter 6, for example, is only dedicated to string, so worry not; we will get there! Here, it is important that you have grasped the concept of a variable and a data type before continuing since they will be the basis for all the programming that you will carry out and for the next steps of this book. As you read throughout this chapter, things will become more clear, and you will understand as I give you more examples to practice on.

## Types of Variables

Java developers need to know three types of variables: **local**, **instance**, and **class**. I have detailed them below with examples to help you understand what they are and what they do.

**Local Variables**

The first type of variable is the **local** variable, which is when a variable is created within a block or a method. This means that it is within the set of keys { and } during the method declaration. It will be automatically created at the block creation and eliminated once you exit it. Because of these characteristics, it will only be accessible to be run in the program within the block in which it exists and, therefore, be "local." Let's look at how this would apply to the code we created.

```
package com.mycompany.projectone;

public class MyFirstClass {

public static void main (String[] args) {

String firstName = "Scott"; //declared local variable

System.out.println("Hello World, Hello " + firstName);

}

}
```

The output once you run the program will be "Hello World, Hello Scott." In our case, the code to print "Scott" was inside the "main" method or within the second set of keys. This means that every time you refer to the string "firstName" in this block, it will refer back to "Scott.'

**Java convention**: Variables should be named in mixed case if its name is composed of more than a word. This means that the initial letter should be capitalized for every new word after the first, which should always be in lowercase. Keep in mind what you are using since Java is case-sensitive. This means that "firstname" will mean something different than "firstName" and "FIRSTNAME." I also cannot have the same name as a keyword or another variable declared within the same scope.

## *Instance Variables*

**Instance** variables are also referred to as **non-static** variables. Different from the local variables, these will be declared outside the method or block; they are generally declared within a class. Just as the local variable will be created and destroyed at the beginning and the end of a method, the same will happen to the instance variable when it refers to the class. To create one, you will need to create an instance of the object and an object itself, even if the default value is zero. Let's take a look at an example with our code:

package com.mycompany.projectone;

public class MyFirstClass {

public String firstName; //declared instance variable

public MyFirstClass () { //default constructor

this.firstName = "Scott"; //use the word this to call for the instance variable

}

public static void main (String[] args) {

MyFirstClass scott= new MyFirstClass (); //this is the creation of the object

System.out.println("Hello World, Hello " + scott.firstName);

}

}

The output here will be the same: "Hello World, Hello Scott." Here, as you can see, some differences and some particularities need to be observed. Let's go through them one by one. The **default constructor** will need to have the same name as the class, as you see in the MyFirstClass repetition and the comments. The word **this** will be needed to represent the instance of the class, meaning "in **this** instance."

Last but not least, in the construction ("Hello World, Hello " + scott.firstName) you see that "scott." was used before "firstName." This is because you need to access the methods or the variables that belong to the object, as in "MyFirstClass scott"—that, in this case, is an accessor.

## *Class Variables*

Opposite to the instance variables, the **class variables** are also known as **static variables**. They are declared similarly to the instance variables, but you need to use the word **static** within the line of code to declare it. These variables are created in the beginning and eliminated at the end of the program. As the word might suggest, when you declare a static variable, it will not move; it will remain the same for all the instances in the same classes. Its default value is also zero.

**Pro tip**: If you do not name the class or the object, the IDE compiler will automatically replace the object name with the name of the class or add the name of the class to the code line.

Let's take a look at an example:

package com.mycompany.projectone;

```java
public class MyFirstClass {

    public static String treatment = "Mr./Mrs."; //declared class variable

    public String firstName;

    public MyFirstClass (String firstName) { // constructor

        this.firstName = firstName; //use the word this to call for the instance variable

    }

    public static void main (String[] args) {

        MyFirstClass scott= new MyFirstClass ("Scott"); //this is the creation of the object

        MyFirstClass steve= new MyFirstClass ("Steve"); //this is the creation of the object

        System.out.println("Hello World, Hello " + scott.treatment + " " +scott.firstName);

        System.out.println("Hello World, Hello " + steve.treatment + " " + steve.firstName);

    }

}
```

Now, in this last example of code, we have added both instance and class variables. The outputs will be "Hello World, Hello Mr./Mrs. Scott" and "Hello World, Hello Mr./Mrs. Steve." Let's take a deeper look at each of them. For the case where I have applied scott.treatment and steve.treatment, you will see that "Mr./Mrs." has been added to the output. This means that independent of the changing variable, that in this case is the instance or non-static variable (the names "Scott" or "Steve" in this case," or any other user name), the static variable will always remain the same (treating the user as "Mr./Mrs.").

## Rules for Naming Variables in Java

Because Java is a strict language, it also has several rules when it comes to naming variables. You have already seen the language convention regarding naming classes and variables, but there are a few more rules you should keep in mind. Keep in mind that having rules on naming is part of all languages, even if the ones I will explain here are applied to Java only. The rules below were extracted from the official Oracle website (2019) and will give you a better idea of what can or cannot be done:

- Java is case-sensible, so beware of what your choice of wording is.

- A variable name can be composed of any identifier with characters in Unicode—letters, special characters, and digits.

- A variable name can start with a letter, the dollar sign, or an underscore character.

- "The convention, however, is to always begin your variable names with a letter, not '$' or '_.' Additionally, the dollar sign character, by convention, is never used at all."

- Blank spaces are not permitted.

- Use common sense to name your variables—avoid using abbreviations so that others can understand what you wanted to say in that part of the code.

- Remember not to use special or reserved keywords.

**Java convention**: "If it consists of more than one word, capitalize the first letter of each subsequent word. If your variable stores a constant value, such as static final int NUM_GEARS = 6, the convention changes slightly, capitalizing every letter and separating subsequent words with the underscore character. By convention, the underscore character is never used elsewhere" (Oracle, 2019, Naming section).

## More Information on Variables

The variables, as you have seen, are an essential part of programming. Without it, you cannot develop simply because they are what will determine what your code should do. Therefore, it is important to understand them to avoid compilation errors before publishing your code. Even though you have already seen the essentials of variables, there are two more concepts important to know before moving on. The first is that variables have a scope and a lifetime. The second is that there are two types of variables, mutable and immutable. These concepts will be important for you to understand because they will determine the type of variable you will use.

### *Variable Scope and Lifetime*

To put it in simple terms, the **scope** of the variable will be the place where it is within the method. For example, if you have a variable written within the class, this means that its scope will be applied to all the elements in that class. If you look at a local variable, for example, you will see that its scope is within the block in which it is declared. This means that it will only work for that block of code within which it was written.

In addition to this, the **lifetime** of the variable will be directly linked to its scope. Essentially, it refers to what instances this variable will begin and end. You might not realize this now, but we approached the variable lifetime when detailing them in the previous section. When I mentioned when the variable would start and be eliminated, this was a direct reference to the lifetime of the variable.

To make things easier, a table elaborated by S. Kumar (n.d., Summary section) will help you fixate the ideas:

| Variable Type | Scope | Lifetime |
| --- | --- | --- |
| Instance variable | Within all classes except in static methods. | Until the object is available in the memory. |

| Class variable | Throughout the class. | Until the end of the program. |
|---|---|---|
| Local variable | Within the block where it was declared. | Until the control leaves the block within which it was declared. |

**Best Practices When Using Variables**

As you already know, it is essential that others understand what you mean when writing code. This can be because you are working in a team or maybe because you might not be taking care of it indefinitely. Another good reason to keep your code easy to read is that you might not touch it for some time and when you get back, you need to understand what you meant at that moment.

For these reasons, the market has established some "good practices" concerning writing variables. These are guidelines that every Java developer should follow, although they are not mandatory. Here is a list of some of the best practices that should be applied when declaring your variables:

1. **Name the variable according to its use**. This means that the name you give it will be as close as possible to what you designed it to do. Avoid abbreviations since not everyone might understand what you mean. In our code, for example, you should not abbreviate "treatment" to "tmt" since the latter would be unknown to most people.

2. **Avoid using the underscore sign "_" to name the variables**. Instead, alternate between capital and lowercase letters, known as "camel case." In our example, "firstName" is better than "first_name.'

3. **Use shorter names to better comprehend**. Long names will make the code unnecessarily extensive and, thus, should be avoided. In our example, we could have used the name "userFirstName," but this would be longer than "firstName', which we have used. In this case, the shorter version still states what you want the variable to do, so there is no need to keep it longer.

4. **Reuse variables**. This will help reduce the memory use of your computer, and it means that you will need to create fewer objects. To reuse a variable, you can just reassign a value to it.

5. **Avoid declaring more than one variable in the same line**. This will make your code complicated and cluttered, leading to mistakes and poor comprehension of your written code. As a best practice, use one line per variable to make understanding and debugging easier.

## Garbage Collector

Most modern languages have a feature called a **garbage collector**. Its main function is to manage the memory while objects are created and eliminated. Once they become needless, the garbage collector will gather them and delete them to make more space in the computer's memory. In Java, the garbage collector is automatic, meaning that the developer does not need to go through the code manually to see what needs to be eliminated. This is one of Java's main features compared to other languages, such as C and C++.

The garbage collector works in what is known as the Java Virtual Machine, or the JVM. The JVM will automatically run it once done by making the reference null, assigning one reference to another, and making it anonymous. This will avoid you from facing memory errors during the compilation, such as the **OutOfMemoryError** (Agarwal & Miglani, 2016).

### *Mutable and Immutable Variables*

Variables can be either mutable (fields can be modified) or immutable (fields cannot be changed after the object is created). According to Pedamkar (2020), when you consider these variables, they will compare with the following characteristics (Head to Head Comparison between Mutable vs Immutable Java section):

| **Mutable** | **Immutable** |
|---|---|
| Java mutable objects can be modified after their creation. | Java immutable objects cannot be modified after their creation. |
| No new object is formed when changes are made to an existing object. | Whenever an existing object is changed, a new object is formed. |
| It provides methods to change the content of an object. | It does not provide methods for changing the content of an object. |
| Getter and setter methods are present in mutable classes. | Only getter methods are present and not setter methods. |
| Mutable classes may or may not be thread-safe. | Immutable classes are thread-safe by default. |
| Some common examples of mutable classes in java are StringBuffer, StringBuilder, and java.util.Date. | All Legacy classes, Wrapper classes, and String classes are common examples of Immutable classes in java. |

Let's take a look at what these variables would look like in our examples.

**Mutable variable**

package com.mycompany.projectone;

public class MyFirstClass {

// Instance Variables (also known as Attributes in OOP)

private String firstName;

private String lastName;

// Constructor with Parameters

MyFirstClass (String firstName, String lastName) {

```java
this.firstName = firstName;
this.lastName = lastName;
}
public String getFirstName(){
return firstName;
}
// this setter can modify the firstName
public void setFirstName (String firstName) {
this.firstName = firstName;
}
//this setter can modify the lastName
public String getLastName() {
return lastName;
}
//this setter can modify the lastName
public void setLastName (String lastName) {
this.lastName = lastName;
}
public static void main(String[] args) {
//Create an object instance
MyFirstClass obj = new MyFirstClass ("Scott" , "Brandt");
System.out.println("First user name is " + obj.getFirstName());
System.out.println("Last user name is " + obj.getLastName());
// update firstName, and lastName as is mutable
obj.setFirstName("Steven");
```

obj.setLastName("Sanders");

System.out.println("Modified user name is " + obj.getFirstName());

System.out.println("Modified user last name is " + obj.getLastName());

}

}

In this case, the output will be:

"First user name is Scott

Last user name is Brandt

Modified user name is Steven

Modified user last name is Sanders"

**Immutable variable**

package com.mycompany.projectone;

public class MyFirstClass {

//variables declared as final cannot be modified

final String firstName;

final String lastName;

public MyFirstClass(String firstName, String lastName) {

this.firstName = firstName;

this.lastName = lastName;

}

public String getFirstName(){

return firstName;

}

public String getLastName() {

return lastName;

}

```
public static void main(String[] args) {
    MyFirstClass obj = new MyFirstClass ("Scott" , "Brandt");
    System.out.println("First user name is " + obj.getFirstName());
    System.out.println("Last user name is " + obj.getLastName());
    //contents cannot be modified
}
}
```

In this case, the output will be:

"First user name is Scott

Last user name is Brandt"

While creating your immutable code, remember that you need to have a public constructor and that there should be no setter methods present for any of the variables. On the other hand, you should define getter methods for all the variables. Keep in mind that you need to use the word "fina" to make it immutable.

**Pro tip**: In Java's version 14, a new data type named Record was introduced. The main reason for this is that when using Java in big data projects, the information needs to be immutable. The Record feature will allow the data to remain immutable without the need to use the word "final" but rather replace it with the record data type. In our case, it would look like this:

```
public record MyFirstClass (String firstName, String lastName) {}
```

This will make your code immutable without needing to write several lines of code for the versions of Java above 14. For the previous versions, you would need to use the word "final" and write the lines of code we have seen before.

Since I have already started giving you more details on data types, read on to see what they are, how to work with them, convert them, and all the information you will need to continue developing your program.

## Working With Data Types in Java

All variables need a data type. The data type is what will determine how much space the variable will take in your memory. In Java, you have two categories of data types, they are **primitive data types** and **non-primitive data types** (also known as an object data type). When you use a primitive data type, this means that you are using a data type that has a predefined value that will be assigned to memory in bytes. Java has eight primitive data types that can be used by the developer.

*The Eight Primitive Data Types in Java*

1. **boolean**: Occupies one bit of memory in the computer and has only two values: true or false. It is considered the most simple data type in Java. The default value for this data type is "false" and operators such as **and**, **or**, **if** can be used in the statement.

   ```
   package com.mycompany.projectone;
   public class MyFirstClass {
   public static void main (String[] args) {
   //first, set the boolean to a true or false—these are the only two possible values
   boolean firstName = true;
   boolean lastName = false;
   //let's suppose we will write an if condition
   if (firstName == true){
   ```

```
System.out.println("Hello World, Hello " + firstName);
}
if (lastName == false){
System.out.println("Hello World, Hello " + lastName);
}
}
}
```

The output in this example would be:

Hello World, Hello Scott

Hello World, Hello Brandt

2. **byte**: This data type will occupy eight bytes of the computer's memory. The most useful application of the byte will be to save memory in large arrays. The values it accepts vary from -128 ($-2^7$) to 127 ($-2^7-1$), but it is important to know that **byte only accepts whole numbers**. The default value for a byte data type is zero.

```
package com.mycompany.projectone;
public class MyFirstClass {
public static void main (String[] args) {
byte days = 100;
//in this case, the values can vary from -128 to 127.
System.out.println(days);
//not that here, we do not use the quotation marks, they are not needed
//for the byte data type, you have established that the name is days
//the printout will be what "days" represents, in this case, 100
}
}
```

The output in this example would be: 100.

3. **char**: This is the abbreviation of the word "character." It uses 16-bit memory (2 bytes) and can be any Unicode character from 0 to 65,535. "When defining our variables, we can use any character literal, and they will get automatically transformed into their Unicode encoding for us. A character's default value is '/u0000'" (Baeldung, 2018, 2.8 char section). The value of the variable, in this case, should be placed within simple quotation marks "and ".

```
package com.mycompany.projectone;

public class MyFirstClass {

public static void main (String[] args) {

char initial = 'S';

//in this case, you will be determining a specific character, most specifically a letter.

System.out.println("Char is equal to: " + initial);

}

}
```

The output will be: Char is equal to S.

4. **double**: Regarding data types, the double will enable you to write decimal numbers. It is stored in 64 bits of memory, allowing longer numbers and, because of this characteristic, it is generally chosen as the standard by developers for writing numbers. The double can have up to 16 decimal digits, and its default value is 0.0. The range considered by double is from $4.9406564584124654 \times 10^{-324}$ to $1.7976931348623157 \times 10^{308}$ both positive and negative. Similar to **float** which we will see next, double was created for scientific calculations that accept approximation errors. To declare a double, you will need to add the letter "d" to the value.

double amount: 5,5748d;

5. **float**: The developer will use float instead of **double** when they want to save memory space when using long numbers. However, here it is important to know that after the sixth decimal number, it will start to lose precision and the result will be more of an estimate than an actual precise result of the calculation. It accepts up to seven decimal numbers, and the default value is 0.0. Also similar to double, you will need to add a letter "f" to the value to declare it appropriately.

   float points: 5,57f;

6. **int**: An abbreviation of "integer," the **int** data type is commonly used for whole numbers and arithmetic operations. When you use this data type, you occupy 32 bits of memory (4 bytes). Its default value is 0. This data type is similar to byte, and the difference is that it occupies more memory.

   int classmates: 23;

7. **long**: As the name might suggest, **long** was created for especially large numbers and is considered an older relative of **int** and this makes it possible to do with it everything you do with int. Because of this property, it occupies 64 bits of memory and is used when the int data type does not support the size of the number. Its default value is zero, and its possible values are between -9,223,372,036,854,775,808($-2^{63}$) and 9,223,372,036,854,775,807 ($2^{63} - 1$).

   long population: 1_234_567_890;

8. **short**: When you need a memory-saving alternative that cannot be as small as a **byte** or as heavy as **int**, you use **short**. Short allows all arithmetic calculations and has a default value of zero. It does the same things as the previously mentioned data types but occupies 2 bytes (16 bits) in the memory. It accepts values from -32,768 ($-2^{15}$) to 32,767 ($2^{15}-1$).

   short cityHomes: 5_792

## How to Convert Between Data Types

When you use Java, you can convert data types to better adjust to the code you are writing. You can convert number data types and character data types to what better adjusts to your needs. Although they are rather simple to carry out, you need to be careful to not create errors or bugs while doing it. Among these can be the loss of precision in the result because the final answer is being cut.

### Converting Numbers to Other Numbers

You can use the conversion from numbers to numbers in two ways: to **widen** the code or **narrow** it. When you widen the code, you are moving from a smaller to a higher precision conversion. This is generally done automatically by the compiler in the IDE. This will happen if the data types are compatible and if we give the value of a smaller data type to a larger one. To make the visualization easier, here is the direction that is followed for conversion in Java:

$$byte \rightarrow short \rightarrow int \rightarrow long \rightarrow float \rightarrow double$$

Let's see how this conversion would work in an example of code.

```java
package com.mycompany.projectone;

public class RankingNumbers {

public static void main (String[] args) {

int a = 50;

long b = a;

float c = b;

//here, you are saying that a = 50, that b = a and that c = b.

//so according to logic, a, which = 50, will be = c, which will also be 50
```

```
System.out.println("Int value: " + a);

System.out.println("Long value: " + b);

System.out.println("Float value: " + c);

}

}
```

The output of your program will, therefore, be:

Int value 50

Long value 50

Float value 50.0

When you **narrow** the code, it will follow the opposite direction of the widening. This means that the flow will be like this:

**double→float→long→int→short→byte**

However, because in this case you are not gaining information, but rather having to decide what to eliminate, reduce, or lose information, you will need to do it manually. Due to this, you will need to write in your code exactly what it is that you want the compiler to do. The following code is an example:

```
package com.mycompany.projectone;

public class RankingNumbers {

public static void main (String[] args) {

double c = 137.06;

long d = (long)c;

int e = (int)d;
```

//here, you are saying that c = 137.06, that d = c and that e = d.

//now, here you need to remember that long and int only accept whole numbers

//therefore, this is what you will run

System.out.println("Double value: " + c);

System.out.println("Long value: " + d);

System.out.println("Int value: " + e);

}

}

The output of your program will be:

Double value 137.06

Long value 137

Int value 1373

## Converting Numbers and Characters

Another possibility that Java offers is to convert characters into numbers and backward. When this happens, you can be converting, for example, **int** to **char** or **char** to **int**. In these examples, the letter you assign will become its equivalent in the ASCII table and the same will happen if you are converting a number to a letter.

package com.mycompany.projectone;

public class Conversion {

public static void main (String[] args) {

char letter = 'g';

int value = letter;

System.out.println(value);

}

}

The output for this will be 103. On the other hand, if you are doing the contrary, the code would look like this:

package com.mycompany.projectone;

public class Conversion {

public static void main (String[] args) {

int value= 103;

char letter = (char) value;

System.out.println(letter);

}

}

The output of the system, in this case, will be "g."

## *Non-Primitive Data Types*

Now that you have already seen the primitive data types on Java, it is time to take a peek at the **non-primitive** or **reference data types**. Although they will be mentioned in this section, we will deep-dive into them in the following chapters of this book. (For easier reference, as I mention them I will name where you can find them.) There are five main types of reference data types: **Class**, **Interface**, **String**, **Array**, and **Object**. These are the native data types for Java, and everything else that is created apart from these will be derived from one of these.

- **Class**: We have been mentioning classes up to now, so I believe that what a class is clear. To have a quick recap, the class will be the blueprint that will be used to create the code by representing real-life objects in the format of this language that will be aggregated and compose the system that you want to create. It will represent the properties that are common to this object. For more information on creating classes, refer to Chapter 3.

- **Interface**: An interface is similar to a class, but when you declare the signatures, they are abstract. An interface can have a method and variables, but it will only say what a class has to do, and not how it will do it. The interface is considered the blueprint of the class. We will learn more about interfaces and their characteristics in Chapter 12.

- **String**: A string is a word that is defined as a series of characters together. In other words, when you have a single letter, you will use char, but when you need to type a word, you will use "String." Essentially speaking, the string is a list of chars. We will approach the subject of strings in the next chapter of this book.

- **Array**: When you use an array in Java, you are using a group of similar data types. They can store primitive and non-primitive data types and allow multiple values to be stored in a single variable. This will be useful when you want to declare all values at the same time instead of independently. An array can be best explained as a collection of variables of the same type. Arrays are used by measuring member length, and they can be declared just as any other variable. Chapter 7 will discuss arrays, their uses, and their applications.

- **Object**: An object is what Java is built upon since it is an OOP language. This means that when you develop, you are making associations with real-life instances. Because of this, everything in Java is an object. You will learn more details on the subject once you reach Chapter 12, which is fully dedicated to the subject.

# Exercise

This chapter gave you a lot of information and to fix it, we are going to do two exercises for which I will guide you in one, and in the other, you will be able to explore for yourself. In each of the sections, I have given you examples of how the variables and data types will apply to the code we are using as an example. I want you to go back and try out all the codes on your computer.

After you are done, and you have ascertained that no mistakes have been made, you should test options within the code. Try using different variables and data types in the code using random information. See if the output is according to what you expected. If you use the same frame and examples, the results should be positive.

The second exercise I want to propose is for you to create a program from scratch. This will enable you to practice creating the packages and classes and all the information you have learned so far. The characteristics of this program are:

Create a "Person" class with the name attributes (string), age (float), place of birth (string), and address (string) in which the age and the place of birth are immutable. You should create a "getAge" method (should return an *int*—make the correct conversion). Create the main method that should have the following as output: *My name is Joe Martin, born in Miami, I'm 35 years old and my address is 12, Sesame St.*

**Tip:** Create an object "Joe" and use the class "Person."

```
package com.smartchat.chat;

public class Person {

private String name;

private final String bornLocale;

private String address;
```

```java
private final float age;

public Person(String name, String bornLocale, String address, float age){

this.name = name;

this.bornLocale = bornLocale;

this.address = address;

this.age = age;

}

public int getAge(){

return (int)age;

}

public static void main (String[] args) ){

Person joe = new Person("Joe Martin", "Miami", "12, Sesame St.", 35.5f);

System.out.println("My name is " + joe.name + ", born in " + joe.bornLocale + ", I'm " + joe.getAge() + " years old and my address is: " + joe.address);

}

}
```

# Summary

In this chapter, you have learned all the information necessary to use variables and data types.

With this, you can already start your career as a developer. You have seen what variables are, their types, uses, and restrictions.

The same can be said for data types. The information you have gained in this chapter will be essential as you move on with your reading since most of the coding in Java will be done by using what was presented here.

Therefore, if you need to, go back, read again, and see if you have assimilated the most important concepts.

Once you have done this, you will be ready to move on to one of the types of non-primitive data types that have been mentioned: strings.

# Chapter 6: Creating and Using Strings in Java

Did you know that strings in Java are immutable, which means they cannot be changed? This can be surprising to some people who are used to other programming languages where strings are mutable. A **string** is used to store a sequence of **char** and, in Java, it is an object. A String can also be a class. In this case, it will be used to create and manage other strings. But let's not get ahead of ourselves.

We will start by taking a look at what a string essentially is when compared to char. For example, let's suppose you want to write the word "study" in your program. If you used char, it would look like this:

```java
public class Main{

public static void main(String args[]){

char[] action = {'s', 't', 'u', 'd', 'y'};

System.out.println(action);

}

}
```

Now, can you imagine what would happen if you needed to write a sentence in your program and the amount of time and effort it would take if you were using char? For this reason, the **string** exists. In this case, instead of writing character by character, you would do the following:

```java
public class Main{

public static void main(String args[]){

String action = "study";

System.out.println(action);
```

}

}

Here, you will notice that while in the char example we used **single quotes**, in the **string** example, double quotes were used around the world that we wanted to print. In both cases, the output was "study," but I guess you can imagine that it took less time to do the second one when compared to the first. If you look back a few chapters, you will see that we have been using string for our examples so far. Every time that we referred to "Scott," we would use a string. The same thing was used in our example at the end of the last chapter.

**Creating Strings in Java**

You might be wondering how a string object can be created when you are using Java. There are two ways to do this: by using a **string literal** or by a **new keyword**. String literal is what we have been using so far: a group of characters that are enclosed by double quotes. On the other hand, we need to use the *new* keyword to create a string. Keep reading to look at two examples:

String bodyPart = "eyes";

//using string literal

String bodyParts = new String ("eyes");

//using new keyword to create string

The advantage of using the string literal is that it will occupy less space within the computer since it will look into a constant pool of words, also known as the **String Constant Pool**. These are stored in Java's heap memory that contains a certain quantity of these words which the JVM looks into when a string is created. Once it is looked up, two things can happen: The word is there, and it is stored in the reference variable or it is not there and a new object is created and stored in the pool for future reference. In this case, the only thing being created is one object.

On the other hand, when you create a new keyword, you create a new string object and a new instance of the String class. You might be thinking that these are the same things but they are not. The main difference here is that while the string literal will create a new word within the pool when you use a new keyword it will be created in the heap memory *outside* the string constant pool.

"All string objects created using the new keyword are allocated space in the heap memory (outside the string constant pool) irrespective of whether the same valued strings are already present in the heap memory or not" (Sufiyan, 2022, By New Keyword section).

## Using Strings in Java

When you use Strings in Java, they are provided by a class named **java.lang.String**. The idea is to make working with Strings easier by applying these methods. When you are creating a program that will process human language, for example, this can be extremely useful as it will enable you to create text in your program. Although the number of options to use String is exhaustive, I do not think it would be productive to add them all, since this would mean pages and more pages of options.

For a general idea, please find below a list with examples of the 10 most common String methods used in Java. (*Observation*: the syntax of each of the methods is placed in parenthesis after its name.)

1. ***Concatenate* (string.concat(the other string))**: Concatenates two strings.

    "Hello ".concat("World");

    Output: Hello World

2. ***Compare* (string.contains(strings you want to compare))**: Compares two strings.

   ```
   class CompareExample{
   public static void main(String args[]){
   String text="Good morning how are you";
   System.out.println(text.contains("Good morning")); //output: true
   System.out.println(text.contains("how are")); //output: true
   System.out.println(text.contains("today")); //output: false
   }
   }
   ```

3. ***Length* (stringName.length())**: Is used to determine the length of the string.

   ```
   "Hello World".length();
   ```

   Output: 11

4. ***Index* (string.indexOf(character you want to see))**: Is used to retain the position of a character within the string you are analyzing.

   ```
   "Hello".indexOf("e");
   ```

   Output: 1

**Pro tip**: Index starts with value zero, which is the first position, this is the reason why the result of the output, in this case, was one.

5. ***Replace character* (string.replace(old character, new character))**: Is a method used to replace a specific character within a string.

   ```
   "Hello".replace("e", "a");
   ```

Output: Hallo

6. ***Uppercase* (string.toUpperCase) and *lowercase* (string.toLowerCase)**: Is used to convert a string into uppercase or lowercase.

"Hello".toUpperCase();

Output: HELLO

"Hello".toLowerCase();

Output: hello

7. ***Split* (string.split(write here the separator you want))**: Is used to split a string into an array of strings.

"Hello World".split(" ");

Output: String[2] = {"Hello", "World"}

8. ***Equals* (string.equals(another string))**: Is used to verify if two determined strings are the same or not.

"Hello ".equals("World");

Output: false

9. ***Join* (string.join(what will join the strings, string 1, string 2))**: Is used to join however many strings you want to put together by using a separator, that will be determined in the beginning of the value.

String.join("_", "Hello", "World", "!");

Output: Hello_World_!

10.    ***Trimming* (string.trim())**: Removes a specific part of the string or white spaces that might exist.

"Hello     ".trim();

Output: "Hello" (with all white spaces removed)

# Exercises

Below you will find a series of exercises to practice your newly acquired string skills.

1. *Write a program to concatenate two strings.*

   String 1: Hi there!

   String 2: How are you?

   The output should be: Hi there! How are you?

2. *Write a program to check if the two strings contain the same data.*

   String 1: "Scott Brandt"

   String 2: "Mike Matthews"

   The output should be: false

3. *Write a program to determine the length of a string.*

   String: "This is my new book on Java"

   Output should be: 27

4. *Write a program to replace one word for another.*

   String: "I ate a red apple today"

   Replace the "apple" with "strawberry"

   The output should be: I ate a red strawberry today.

5. *Write a program to convert all the characters into uppercase and then use the resulting string to write them all as lowercase.*

   String: "Run, ThE sTOrm IS ComINg!"

Output in uppercase: RUN! THE STORM IS COMING!

Output in lowercase: run! the storm is coming!

# Summary

This chapter has taught you all about strings. You have learned that strings are immutable and are a sequence of char.

One of the main things you should remember is that while with a char you will use single quotation marks when you want to give a value to the string, it should be placed within double quotation marks.

Additionally, you have learned how to create strings—with a string literal or a new keyword—and also some of the methods that can be applied to them.

You are now able to edit the text within your programs and this will take you a step further.

In the next chapter, you will learn about another non-primitive variable that is essential for Java developers to know: arrays.

# Chapter 7: Using Arrays in Java

Arrays are a very important part of Java as they allow you to store and manipulate data in a concise and efficient manner. The main reason for this is that an array will allow you to store several values within the same variable. Adding more than one value to a single variable will enable you to have a shorter and cleaner code, making it easier for others who will read what you wrote. There are many different types of arrays that you can use when developing with Java, each with its own benefits and drawbacks. Read on to learn more.

**What Is an Array?**

An array is a data structure that stores a collection of elements of the same type. When an array is created, its length will be determined and fixed. To access any element within the array, you will need to use its index, where the first position is always zero, and not one. This is what an array will look like:

`int position[] = new int[5];`

In this case, "position" is the name of the array. As you have learned in the previous chapters, this array uses an integer, meaning that it will store whole numbers. The number five represents the size of the array, which will be important because of its index-based characteristics. In our example, the first index would be zero and the fifth index would be four.

You might be thinking that you have seen this before—and you are right! You have! When you use the String "split" function, your result will be an array, for example. The same example can be applied if you are using a series of char as we used in this situation `char[] action = {'s', 't', 'u', 'd', 'y'};`. Look at this example we have for "study." In this case, "s" is index zero, "t" is index one, and so on.

Among the advantages of using an array is the optimization of your code and the ability to have access to any data by using the index feature. On the other hand, it presents a disadvantage because since the array is fixed, we can only store within it the elements that "fit" in it, disabling it to grow in size when you run the code.

**How to Create an Array in Java**

To create an array in Java, you need to use the "new" keyword followed by the data type. You will use one of the methods you have already seen to specify the type of data that you are creating and this needs to be followed by the square brackets "[]."

When we are declaring an array, the syntax that needs to be followed is *method, bracket with the number of indexes, name, the equal sign, and next the array*. To make the example more visual, let's look again at the previous example:

char[] actions = new char[5];

char[] action = {'s', 't', 'u', 'd', 'y'};

Here, as you will be able to see, we have the following:

dataType [] arrayName = new dataType [size]

Or, in one step:

dataType [size] action = {elements}

You have now created and declared an Array in Java.

**How to Use an Array in Java**

Once you have created an array, you can access and modify its elements using the index. Let's use a practical example to make things more visual. Here, we will give the program a series of names and ask it to print out one in the index place number 2. This is what it will look like:

```java
package com.mycompany.projectone;
public class UsingArray {
public static void main (String[] args) {
String[] myListOfNames = {"Scott", "Steve", "Sam", "Sophia", "Scarlett"};
System.out.println("My best friend's name is: "+ myListOfNames[2]);
}
}
```

The output, in this case, will be: *My best friend's name is: Sam.*

# Exercise

For the exercise section of this chapter, I want you to create an array. The specifications of the program I want you to create are:

- Create a new Java project in Eclipse.
- Create a new class in the project and name it Main.
- In the Main class, create a new array of type int called numbers with 10 elements.
- Initialize the array with the numbers 1 through 10.
- Print out the contents of the array.

**Solution:**

```
package com.mycompany.projectone;

public class ExerciseUsingArray {

public static void main (String[] args) {

int[] number={1,2,3,4,5,6,7,8,9,10};

System.out.println("number[0] = " + number[0]); //output: 1

System.out.println("number[1] = " + number[1]); //output: 2

System.out.println("number[2] = " + number[2]); //output: 3

System.out.println("number[3] = " + number[3]); //output: 4

System.out.println("number[4] = " + number[4]); //output: 5
```

```java
System.out.println("number[5] = " + number[5]); //output: 6

System.out.println("number[6] = " + number[6]); //output: 7

System.out.println("number[7] = " + number[7]); //output: 8

System.out.println("number[8] = " + number[8]); //output: 9

System.out.println("number[9] = " + number[9]); //output: 10

	}

}
```

# Summary

Now that you understand and know what an array is, it will be easier to simplify your code when developing a program.

You have seen that an array is a set of data of the same type that can be identified by an index that will save you some memory space when using your computer.

After reading this chapter, you already have the basics of Java coding and can even start writing your programs as a test. If you need to, take a break, go back a few chapters, and re-read the information.

If you feel that you have all the information you need, congratulations! You are doing very well!

As we move on to the next chapter, we will start getting into more detail on how to use decision-makers and operators in Java.

Keep in mind that the concepts you have learned so far need to be clear, as we will be using them in the examples on how to use the aforementioned tools. Ready?

Let's go!

# Chapter 8: Using Operators and Decision-Making in Java

Operators are important in Java because they allow you to perform actions on variables and data. With them, you will be able to perform comparisons and arithmetic operations and apply logic to your code. These are a few essential elements that will need to be added since most of the time a program is not static and needs to adapt to certain conditions according to what the user does.

This brings us to the next item of the chapter, which is decision-making tools. Decision-making is also important in Java, as it allows you to control the flow of your program. These will allow the program to "react" according to the commands that the user requests and how the program will respond to them.

To start off, let's take a look at operators, what they are, how they work, and each of the types that can be used in Java.

## Learning About Operators in Java and How to Use Them

Operators in Java are symbols that perform operations in your values and variables. They are divided into six types: **arithmetic**, **assignment**, **comparison**, **logical**, **bitwise**, and **miscellaneous operators**. Let's take a closer look at what each one is and does.

### *Arithmetic Operators*

The arithmetic operators will be used to perform, as you might have guessed, arithmetic operations in the code. These are the operators that can be used:

| Arithmetic Operator | Function |
|---|---|
| + | Adds two variables or connects two strings. |
| - | Subtracts variables |
| * | Multiplies variables |
| / | Divides variables |
| % | Find the remaining value after a division of variables |

Let's take a look at an example:

```java
package com.mycompany.projectone;

public class ExerciseUsingOperators {

public static void main(String[] args) {

int classrooms = 25;

int boys = 138;

int girls = 162;

double highestGrade = 8.17;

double lowestGrade = 5.68;

// you want to know how many students there are in total: add boys and girls

System.out.println("Total number of students is: " + (boys + girls));

//output: 300

//you want to know many more girls there are

System.out.println("Difference between genders is: " + (girls - boys) +"more girls");

//output: 24

//you want to divide the total number of students per class

System.out.println("Students per class: " + ((girls + boys) / classrooms));

//output: 12

//you want to find the average grade
```

System.out.println("Average grade: " + (highestGrade + lowestGrade) / (2));

//output: 6.925

//you want to find the remainder of the average

System.out.println("Deviation: " + (highestGrade + lowestGrade) % (2));

//output: 1.8499999999999996

}

}

## Assignment Operators

Assignment operators will be used in Java expressions to attribute an assigned value. The operators that can be used are:

| Assignment Operator | Translation |
| --- | --- |
| = | One variable or value equals the other. |
| += | The value of the variable is its attributed value plus the value of the other. |
| -= | The value of the variable is its attributed value times the value of the other. |
| *= | The value of the variable is its attributed value times the value of the other. |
| /= | The value of the variable is its attributed value divided by the value of the other. |
| %= | The value of the variable is its attributed value with the remainder of the other. |

Let's see their application in an example:

package com.mycompany.projectone;

public class ExerciseUsingOperators {

public static void main(String[] args) {

```java
int number = 5;

int test;

// assign value using =

test = number;

System.out.println("Result 1 using =: " + test); //output: 5

// assign value using +=

test += number;

System.out.println("Result 2 using +=: " + test); // output: 10

// assign value using -=

test -= number:

System.out.println("Result 3 using -=: " + test); //output: 5

// assign value using *=

test *= number;

System.out.println("Result 4 using *=: " + test); //output: 25

// assign value using /=

test /= number;

System.out.println("Result 5 using /=: " + test); //output: 5
    }
}
```

## *Comparison or Relational Operators*

As the name might suggest, a comparison operation is used to compare variables and statements. They are mainly composed of mathematical symbols that will allow your program to do exactly what they do when used in mathematics.

| Comparison Operator | Translation |
|---|---|
| == | Equals |
| != | Does not equal |
| > | Greater than |
| < | Less than |
| >= | Greater than or equal to |
| <= | Less than or equal to |

In an example, this would look like:

package com.mycompany.projectone;

public class ExerciseUsingOperators {

public static void main(String[] args) {

int girls = 162, boys = 138;

System.out.println(girls == boys); //output: false

System.out.println(girls != boys); //output: true

System.out.println(girls > boys); //output: false

System.out.println(girls < boys); //output: true

System.out.println(girls >= boys); //output: false

System.out.println(girls <= boys); //output: true

}

}

*Logical Operators*

Logical operators are used to expressing "and," "or," and "not" expressions in Java. Let's see what they are:

| Logical Operator | Translation |
| --- | --- |
| && | And—if both expressions are true. |
| \|\| | Or—if either expression is true. |
| ! | Not—true if the expression is false and false if the expression is true. |

Here is an example:

```
package com.mycompany.projectone;
public class ExerciseUsingOperators {
public static void main(String[] args) {
System.out.println((100>40) && (254<146)); //output: false
System.out.println((100<40) && (254<146)); //output: false
System.out.println((100>40) || (254>146)); //output: true
System.out.println((100<40) || (254<146)); //output: false
System.out.println((100<40) || (254>146)); //output: true
System.out.println(!(100==50)); //output: true
System.out.println(!(100>50)); //output: false
}
}
```

## *Bitwise Operators*

When you apply a bitwise operator, you are asking Java to perform operations on individual bits. Because of these characteristics, I can say they are not commonly used when developing code. These are the operators that can be used:

| Bitwise Operator | Translation |
| --- | --- |
| ~ | Inverts the value of each bit: from 0 to 1 and from 1 to 0 |

| << | Left shift |
|---|---|
| >> | Right shift |
| >>> | Undersigned right shift |
| & | AND in a bit spectrum |
| ^ | OR in a bit spectrum |

## *Misc Operators*

There are several other operators that exist in Java that do not fit any of these classifications. These include **instanceof, comma, member access,** and **ternary** operators, among others.

**Decision-Making in Java**

When you have a code and you apply statements to it, the logical line of thought is that these will be executed in the order they appear. This means that the program will be executed and the calculations carried according to the order in which they were placed, making it essential to ensure that you have correctly placed it. However, since a program is a living entity and it will perform according to certain decisions, it needs to be flexible to respond based on the conditions which they are given. This means that when in one instance you will need to add certain values, in others, it is possible that you have to subtract them depending on the command that was given.

To make this work in Java, it has what is known as **decision-making statements**.

They are composed of four classes: those that belong to the **if statement** (if statement, if-else statement, and else-if statement), **conditional operators**, **switch case statements**, and **miscellaneous statements**. Since we have already seen the conditional operators in the previous section of this chapter, we will not address them again. Here we will learn about the other components of decision-making: those that belong to the if statement, the switch case statement, and the miscellaneous statements.

## *If Statement*

Considered the most simple statement in Java, the **if statement** will be used under the condition that "if this, then that." The syntax of this would be as follows:

if(expression)

{statement a;

statement b;

statement c

}

In an example, this would look like the example below:

package com.mycompany.projectone;

public class UsingIf {

public static void main(String[] args) {

int a = 1, b = 2;

if (a<b);

System.out.println("a is smaller"); //output: a is smaller

if (a>b);

System.out.println("false"); //output: false

}

}

As you have seen in the example above, we have used two if statements. While it is acceptable to use one in some situations if you have more than one condition you can use more than one statement. In this case, they are called **nested if statements**.

*If-Else Statement*

The if-else statement will serve as an additional step to the if statement. In this case, the logic will be: "if this, then that, if not, then other" as shown below by using the same values as before:

```java
package com.mycompany.projectone;

public class UsingIf {

public static void main(String[] args) {

int a = 1, b = 2;

if (a>b){

System.out.println("a is greater");

}

else {

System.out.println("false"); //output: false

}

}

}
```

## Else-if Statement

An **else-if** statement is also known as an if-else-if statement because it will use all three statements in your condition. They are similar to the else statements but differ in the fact that each "else" can be paired with a different "if," giving the program a series of choices for the user. In this case, one condition will happen if the other and based on the decisions made as you can see in the following example.

```java
package com.mycompany.projectone;

public class UsingIf {

public static void main(String[] args) {

int c = 3, d = 3;

if (c>d) {

System.out.println("c is greater");

}

else if (d>c) {

System.out.println("d is greater");

}

else {

System.out.println("They are equal");

}

}

}
```

The output for this situation will be: They are equal.

## Switch Case Statement

The **switch case statement** is a variation of the if and if-else statements. While they will have almost the same function, by using the switch case statement, you will not need to write an "else" for each of the statements that you have. This means you can use a statement with several possibilities and still have the same outcome as if you were using the if and the else, only in a more compressed way, saving you time and energy from writing large amounts of code.

```java
public class Sample {

public static void main(String args[]) {

int number = 4;

switch (number) {
case 1:
System.out.println("The number is one");
break;
case 2:
System.out.println("The number is two");
break;
case 3:
System.out.println("The number is three");
break;
case 4:
System.out.println("The number is four");
break;
default:
System.out.println("No available option. Enter a no between 1 and 4");
```

```
break;
    }
  }
}
```

The output of this program will be: The number is four.

## *Miscellaneous Statements*

The other form of statements are also known as **jump statements**. They are composed of the **break** statement, the **continue** statement, and the **return** statement. The main actions for these are:

- **Break**: To create a break in the workflow of a program such as a loop, as we will see in the next chapter.

- **Continue**: To skip a certain requirement for the program to keep running and avoid a certain action.

- **Return**: To go back and return the control of the program back to the method from which it came.

**Pro tip**: Note that "if we mention the return statement in the main method, the compiler halts and the program comes to an end. None of the statements below the return statement are executed by the compiler" (Data Flair Team, 2018, c. Return Statement in Java section).

**Exercise**

- Try using operators and decision-making in Java to solve a problem.

- Create a project that uses operators and decision-making.

- Practice using the various operators and decision-making statements.

# Summary

This chapter has taught you all about Java operators and decision-makers.

You have seen the operators that can be used while developing your code and how to apply them to different situations.

Based on the information you have here, your programs are becoming more complex. You can code to make a program make decisions based on the conditions that you have established and you can also make it go through a decision-making process.

These tools will be essential for you to know, as you will soon see.

In the next chapter, you'll see the uses of decision-making statements when applying control flow. You will learn about the importance of establishing a control flow chart to map your operations. The main reason for this was mentioned at the beginning of this chapter: The order of statements in Java matters, and you are about to understand why.

# Chapter 9: Control Flow Statements

Control flow statements are important because they allow you to control the order in which your code is executed. This can be useful for making decisions, repeating code, or jumping to a different section of code. Java has several different types of control flow statements that you can use to write more efficient, concise, and optimized code.

## All About Control Flow Statements

When Java developers are building a program, they use what are called **control flow statements** to decide the order in which the programs should run. These are essential because they will determine the order in which each of the blocks of code will run and, because of this, can be considered one of the most important parts of programming in Java. Using control statements will enable you to place decision-making in your program and using them can make your code more complex, especially when they are combined.

*Types of Control Flow Statements*

There are three types of control flow statements. They are **decision-making statements**, **loop statements**, and **jump statements**. In this section, we will take a closer look at what each of these does and what they are generally used for.

**Decision-Making Statements**
**Decision-making** statements are the same as we have already seen in the previous chapter. They are composed of the **if-statement**, the **if-else statement**, and the **switch statement**. Here, there are no differences from what has already been explained. If you have any doubts or questions regarding how they work, please refer to Chapter 8, in the **decision-making section**, to obtain more information. Additionally, since I have already

provided you with examples of these situations, I will not repeat them in the example section of this chapter.

## Loop Statements

**Loop statements** have within their scope three different possibilities: the **for loop,** the **while loop**, and the **do-while loop**. As the name suggests, when you apply this condition to your code, you will request that the same action continues to go on and on again, repeating the same instructions, until there is a piece of code that determines it to stop.

## The For Loop

The **for loop** is a way to write your Java code concisely. It is used when you have a collection and you want to execute a block of code over it or when you want to execute the same code more than a specific number of times. When you have a for loop, you will have three statements: the initialization, the condition, and the increment. Let's take a look at an example below.

```java
public class Example {

public static void main(String[] args) {

int sum = 0; // initialization expression

for(int j = 1; j<=100; j++) { //condition expression and increment expression

sum = sum + j;

}

System.out.println("If you add all the numbers from 1 to 100 the answer is " + sum);

}

}
```

Output: If you add all the numbers from 1 to 100, the answer is 5050.

## The While Loop

Developers usually use the **while loop** as a control flow statement to test if a condition is true until it is proven to be false. In this case, the condition should be repeatedly executed in the block of code by using a Boolean condition. This loop is composed of a test expression and an update expression. An example of this code would look like this:

```java
public class Example{

public static void main(String[] args) {
```

```java
int i = 1; // initial statement

System.out.println("The list of odd numbers from 1 to 10 is: \n");

while(i<=10) { //condition check

System.out.println(i);

i = i + 2; //update expression

}

}

}
```

The output will be: *The list of odd numbers from 1 to 10 is:*

1

3

5

7

9

**The Do-While Loop**

Lastly, there is the **do-while** loop, which is also known as a loop for exit control. In this repetition structure, the block of code will be executed before the condition is tested. It is used when the developer needs to execute the code at least once before conducting the condition testing.

```java
public class Example{

public static void main(String[] args) {

int i = 1; //initial statement

System.out.println("The list of odd numbers from 1 to 10 is: \n");

do {

System.out.println(i);

i = i + 2; //update expression
```

}while(i<=10); //condition check

}

}

The output will be: The list of odd numbers from 1 to 10 is:

1

3

5

7

9

Here, you will note that while the code is similar to the while loop, it is actually the **condition check** that is located in another place of the code. In this case, it is **after** the body of code for the update expression. Therefore, as you can see, first the statement is declared, and only after this, the condition is checked to see if it is true or false.

## Jump Statements

You already know that when you are a developer, you need your code to flow in a certain order so that the actions are carried out in an orderly manner. However, the software is not all linear and you may need to move from one part of the code to the other by skipping a certain part of what was written. For these cases, we use what are called **jump statements**.

Jump statements are syntaxes you place within your code that can interrupt the flow of a program or a specific block of code. It can allow you to leave a loop or continue the processing of information according to the conditions that were established. There are three types of statements in this category: **break statement**, **continue statement**, and **return statement**. Let's look into each of these in more detail.

## The Break Statement

The **break statement** is generally used to leave a loop and for this reason, it is associated with one of the three statements we have seen before. The statement will be applied even if the declared condition is not achieved. Another characteristic of the break statement is that they "are usually used with decision-making statements" (Programiz, n.d.-a). Using the same example we did in the previous section, let's see what the break statement would look like.

public class g {

```java
public static void main(String[] args) {
for(int i = 1; i<= 10; i++) { //statement
System.out.println(i);
if(i==7) { //decision-making statement
break; //break label
}
}
}
}
```

The output of this example will be a list of numbers from 1 to 7 since 7 is the number we have indicated as the stop point of the loop. Here you will note that the break label was applied outside the loop syntax.

**The Continue Statement**

The **continue statement** is different from the break statement for two reasons: The first is that it will only work if it is inside the loop and the second is that applying will make the program "skip" all the lines of code that comes after it. It will have different behaviors if it is in the for or in the while and do-while loops. According to Tutorials Point (n.d.-b), "In a for loop, the continue keyword causes control to immediately jump to the update statement. In a while loop or do/while loop, control immediately jumps to the Boolean expression."

```java
public class ContinueExample{
public static void main(String[] args) {
for(int i=1; i<=10;i++)
{
if (i==5)
{
```

```
continue; //continue label

}

System.out.println(i);

}

}

}
```

Output: In this case, the answer will be a list of numbers from 1 to 10 without the number 5, since we have told the program that if i=5, then it should be skipped and the loop continues to run. In this example, you can see that the continue label was applied inside the loop statement.

## The Return Statement

The **return statement** is also used in association with decision-making statements to return a value after the block of code has completed its execution. Now, do you remember that list of keywords that I gave you in the beginning and said it would be interesting to memorize? Well, if you look back at it, you will see that the word "return" is among one the words on the list. Its use in the return statement is exactly the reason why you cannot use it in your code.

```
public class ReturnStatementExample1{

public static void main(String[] args) {

int age = 25;

System.out.println("Allowed to drink");

if (age>21)

Return;

System.out.println("Not allowed to drink");

}

}
```

Output: Allowed to drink. The answer will be that we have determined that the age we are using is 25. You could apply this when determining a limit, establishing what is greater, and other examples that will require the program to "think" and give you back the answer. For example, if you wanted to find out what is the largest number between two options, you could use the return option as follows:

```java
public class ReturnExample2{
public int compareInt(){ //declare the method in the following lines
int a = 589647821;
int b = 45897128;
System.out.println("a = " + a + "\nb = " + b);
if(a>b) //decision-making statement
return a;//what you want to return
else //decision-making statement
return b; //what you want to return
}
public static void main(String ar[])
{
ReturnExample2 obj = new ReturnExample2();
int result = obj.compareInt();
System.out.println("The greater number among a and b is: " + result);
}
}
```

The output, in this case, will be as follows:

a = 589647821

b = 45897128

The greater number among x and y is: 589647821

# Exercise

As a practice exercise for this section, I want you to create flow charts that represent the flux of information in a code.

This means that you will read the explanation given to you in this chapter and build a flow chart of how the information should flow if the statement is *true* or if the statement is *false*.

This will enable you to visualize the structure for each of the statements previously presented and how it will impact your program.

# Summary

In this chapter, you have learned all about the control flow statements used in Java and how they can be applied in your code to make your program run smoother.

You saw that in most cases, they are not used on their own, but are associated with decision-making statements and other conditions.

If you have any doubts about how to use any of these, my suggestion is to go back and read them again and do some practice exercises on your compiler until you are sure you understand how each of them works.

Next, we will discuss how to create methods in Java, one of the most essential skills you need to know to have a successful coding experience.

# Chapter 10: Creating Methods in Java

If you want to become a Java programmer, it is essential to know how to create methods. Methods allow you to reuse code and make your code more readable and organized. In this chapter, you will learn the basics of methods in Java so that you can start using them in your own projects!

**Methods in Java**

When you need a program to perform a certain task, you need to create what is called a **method**. In all the previous examples that we have seen, a method was created to determine what the code was supposed to do, such as count numbers. Therefore, we can say that a grouped block of code that is created to perform a specific function is a method. One of the advantages of using methods is that they can be reused for different functions within the program, being applied to different contexts while you are programming.

When you want to use a method, there are two ways to go on about it: the first is to create your own method based on the requirements that you have for that specific action and the other is to use one of the available methods in the Java libraries you are using. These methods can be run automatically or then can be only executed when requested, this will depend on your developing approach.

*Why Use Methods?*

Methods can be created or used for several reasons. Two of them are for a better understanding of the code and separating them into blocks so that each method has one objective. In addition to this, applying methods makes your coding more efficient and readable since, when you implement them, it allows your code to be broken into different sections. When you break down the code into several smaller parts, it will be better to identify errors and debug them when necessary. Finally, methods are used to enhance the modifications when they are needed, also known as **maintainability**.

When the code is reusable and is generally the same throughout, it will enable the developer to save time, changing only the parameters that are applied. Parameters are the variables that are applied within the code lines after the method has been declared. Let's take a look at an example.

```
public class Example {
public static void main(String[] args) {
int sum = 0; // declaration of method "SUM"
for(int j = 1; j<=100; j++) {//parameters
sum = sum + j;
}
System.out.println("If you add all the numbers from 1 to 100 the answer is " + sum);
}
}
```

In this example that I have extracted from the previous chapter, you will see by the comments that the name of the method is "sum." In this case, this is a pre-existing method that asks the program to sum the numbers that we will later determine. In this case, I have used a standard method, but what should be done if you want to create your own method in Java?

### *How to Create Methods in Java*

If you are working on a program and your idea is to create your own method for any reason, you will need to build a user-defined method that can be changed depending on the requirement you have for your program. These will be methods that are not available in the Java class libraries (JCL) as happens with methods such as length(), print(), and sqrt().

To create your own method, first, you need to understand that a method is composed of two separate parts: the method **signature** and the method **body**. The body of the method is composed of the code that performs a task while the signature is composed of four different parts. They are:

1. The visibility assessor of the method can be public, private, default, or protected.
2. What do you want the method to return?
3. The name of the method, which can also be called in other parts of the code.
4. The parameter list that is necessary to execute the code within the method.

One important thing to remember is that a method always needs to be created within a class for it to work. In addition to this, once you name the method, you will need to open and close the parenthesis after it. To exemplify, let's use the previous example once more.

```
public class Situation{ //class declaration, in this case, the name is Situation
public int subtractNumbers (int a, int b){//method "subtractNumbers" created
int subtract = a - b; //declares what the method will do
return subtract; //determine what the method has to return back to you
}
public static void main(String[] args) {//creating a method
int c = 128;
int d = 75;
Situation obj = new Situation(); //creating an object of the situation class
int outcome = obj.subtractNumbers(c, d); // call the method we created before
System.out.println("The answer is " + outcome);
}
}
```

The output, in this case, will be: The answer is 53. It is important to note that the name of the class, in this case, "Situation," has to be the same name as the object you are creating so that the program identifies what you are trying to do. In addition to this, you have used the signs that we have seen in previous chapters to perform the mathematical operation we desired, which in this case was a subtraction.

Now that you understand the **user-defined** and the **library methods**, we can move along and take a look at two more Java method types: static and non-static.

**Types of Methods in Java**

Other than the user-defined and library methods, methods in Java can also be divided into static and non-static. To better understand these, we can simply say that static methods are associated with a class, while non-static methods are associated with an object. While static methods can be called without an instance of the class, non-static methods must be called with an instance of the class.

In the **static method**, you need to link it with an instance of a class and cannot be more than one static method class. The static method will determine the behavior of the class that you are creating and, for this reason, it is also known as the class method. When you use the static method, you will only refer to static classes and variables that are within those lines of code you have written.

On the other hand, the **non-static method**, also known as the instance method, *does not* need to be linked to a class instance, but it needs to be connected to an object. This is because it represents what the object will do within the declared method. When it is applied, it can refer to any static method or variable within our code with the need for an object to be created.

To make it visual, let's put it this way:

- Static method: linked to a class.

- Non-static method: linked to an object.

Referring back to our example for this chapter, we have the following:

public class Situation{ //**non-static method declaration**

public int subtractNumbers (int a, int b){

int subtract = a - b;

return subtract; //determine what the method has to return back to you

}

public static void main(String[] args) {//**static method declaration**

int c = 128;

int d = 75;

Situation obj = new Situation();

int outcome = obj.subtractNumbers(c, d); // call the method we created before

System.out.println("The answer is " + outcome);

}

}

## The Basics of Methods in Java

When you have a method in Java, there are several actions that are related to its use. They are **declaring** a method, **invoking** a method, and **returning a value** from a method. Each of these actions means something different and serves different purposes in your code.

## Declaring a Method

When you declare a method in Java, you can only do so inside a specific class. Remember in the previous section, at the beginning of the chapter, when I mentioned the four components of a method? Well, you will need to add two more to declare a method, since it is composed of six parts. These parts added together will provide the system the information on what you want to do. Let's refresh our minds. The method is composed of the following:

1. Access specifier: public
2. Return: return subtract;
3. Method name: subtractNumbers
4. Parameter list: (int a, int b)

And the two new components:

5. Method signature: public int subtractNumbers (int a, int b){
6. Method body: everything that is within the { } after the method signature

**Java convention**: The name of the method should be applied according to what it will do so that other developers who read your code can understand what you mean and what you want to do with it. In our case, since we wanted to subtract, the name that needed to be specified for the method was pretty clear. In this case, it would not make sense to write anything other than this.

**Pro tip**: When you consider a method signature in Java, the action to return is not considered to be part of the signature.

## Invoking a Method

Invoking a method can also be referred to as calling a method. This means that you are going to ask it to execute its task within the program. In our example, we call the method by writing the following: System.out.println("The answer is " + outcome);. Generally speaking, to call the method, you will add an action followed by a parenthesis and a semicolon. In this case, if you use the same method repeatedly, it will bring as output the number of times you have placed it in the code.

For example:

```java
public class Situation{ //non-static method declaration
public int subtractNumbers (int a, int b){
int subtract = a - b;
return subtract; //determine what the method has to return back to you
}
public static void main(String[] args) {//static method declaration
int c = 128;
int d = 75;
Situation obj = new Situation();
int outcome = obj.subtractNumbers(c, d); // call the method we created before
System.out.println("The answer is " + outcome);
System.out.println("The answer is " + outcome);
System.out.println("The answer is " + outcome);
System.out.println("The answer is " + outcome);
System.out.println("The answer is " + outcome);
}
}
```

In this case, the output will be:

The answer is 53

The answer is 53

The answer is 53

The answer is 53

The answer is 53

Because we have invoked the method 5 times within our block of code.

***Returning a Value From a Method***

The return method will be the command you give the program to determine what you want the output to be. In our example, we used return subtract; because what we wanted was for the program to give us the result of subtraction. This was only possible because we used a variable of the *int* type. If we had used, for example, a *string* variable to return a subtraction, our program would give us an error message.

**Pro tip**: "If the method does not return any value, we use the void keyword as the return type of the method" (Programiz, n.d.-b).

# Advanced Methods in Java

When we talk about Java, we need to consider that there are several additional features that an experienced developer will have because of their honed skills. One of the things they do is use what is called **method overloading**. This means that there will be more than one method and each one will have a different parameter. This enables the developer to save up resources and make his code more concise and clean, saving time and making it more efficient to read.

When you use method overloading, there are two ways you can configure the code: The first is to use several parameters with different tasks and the other is to change the data that is contained within the parameter specification. Imagine, for example, that you have a situation in which you need to first subtract two numbers and then multiply them by another to get a result. While you could perfectly do this by using two methods, when you add two of them to a class, it will make the code block easier to manage.

Suppose we have the following:

```
public class Main {

static int plusOverloadAdd(int a, int b, int c) {//method 1

return a + b + c;

}

static int plusOverloadMultiply(int a, int c) {//method 2

return a * c;

}

public static void main(String[] args) {

int myNum1 = plusOverloadAdd(5, 9, 6);

double myNum2 = plusOverloadMultiply(5, 6);//note that here we used double

System.out.println("sum: " + myNum1);

System.out.println("product: " + myNum2);

}

}
```

The output in this case will be:

Sum:20 product 30.0.

By this example, you can see that we call two methods and we add them to one "Main" class. Instead of having several lines of code to reach one conclusion, since we are using the same variables, it is possible to compile it into one, making the code more readable and minimizing its complexity.

# Exercise

Now that you know all about methods, let's practice with two simple exercises.

1. Use Java methods to obtain the average of 5 numbers; numbers 1, 3, 5, 7, and 9.

**Solution**:

```
public class Average1 {
public static void main(String[] args){
double a = 1;
double b = 3;
double c = 5;
double d = 7;
double e = 9;
System.out.print("The average value is " + average(a, b, c, d, e));
}
 public static double average(double a, double b, double c, double d, double e)
{
return (a + b + c + d + e) / 5;
}
}
```

**Output**: The average value is 5.0

2. 
```
public class Concat {
public static void main(String[] args){
String salut = "Hello ";
String name = "Scott";
System.out.print(salutation(salut,name));
```

```
}
    public static String salutation(String salut, String name)
    {
    return salut.concat(name);
    }
}
```

**Output**: Hello Scott

# Summary

You now have all the tools that will enable you to create methods in Java.

Remember that when coding, you can use methods that are available in the JCL or you can create your own methods based on your needs.

To make your code simpler and easier to read, try using overloading methods.

In the next chapter, we will learn more about why Java is considered an object-oriented language and what benefits this characteristic gives it.

# Chapter 11: Object-Oriented Programming in Java

Although it is not required, many developers use OOP when working with Java. This paradigm can help make code more robust and easier to understand. In addition, it can also lead to more efficient applications. When you use OOP, you are implementing different concepts such as inheritance and polymorphism, which we will see later in this chapter and the book. By using OOP, you can grant real-life attributes to programs and create and reuse methods (Great Learning Team, 2021a).

**What Is OOP?**

OOP is a programming paradigm that tries to represent objects from the real world by observing their properties and behaviors and applying them to software. To do this, developers use **classes** and **objects** within the code to design what they want the program to behave like. By associating the code with common objects, those creating the software can better characterize and control the code. "OOP is the most popular programming paradigm used for software development and is taught as the standard way to code for most of a programmer's educational career" (Doherty, 2020, para. 1). Java is only one of the languages that use this approach, other examples can be seen in Python, PHP, Javascript, and C++.

In Java, the OOP is standardized with a set of what is called **principles** or concepts. These are the base of the language—what characterizes and makes it different from others. While there is some divergence among specialists on how to divide each of them, the most accepted explanation is that **classes**, **objects**, **methods**, and **attributes** are part of its main characteristics, the pillars that make it what it is, and concepts, which are divided into **inheritance**, **polymorphism**, **abstraction**, **encapsulation**, **association**, **aggregation**, and **composition**. Let's take a look at each of these.

Since we have already mentioned classes, objects, methods, and attributes in the previous chapters, I won't get into too much detail but rather give a quick overview. Next, we will look at the concepts and what each of these means in Java.

*Pillars*

- **Classes**: These are data types defined by the user. The "blueprint" that the code will be built upon is a part of the logic of the code that is not associated with any real-life item. For example, we could say that a class is "Cats," although we are not specifying what types of cats. They are just the general category to which they belong, and we are not saying if they are tigers, lions, house cats, and so on.

- **Objects**: As you might imagine by the name, objects are the essence of the OOP and Java, in this case. They are most widely known as instances containing the information, or the data, that will be used in the code as its behavior or within the method. In this case, the state of the object for the class cat can be name, color, size, and their behaviors, such as meowing, scratching, and sleeping. In this case, the behaviors are known as methods.

- **Methods**: When you have a method in Java, you are talking about this object's actions. In our case, for the cats, it is simply the actions they carry out, as you have seen mentioned in the explanation of the object. When you have a method, it can give you information on an object and is defined in the class. We can say that the class cat has an object named Scarlet with a scratching method.

- **Attributes**: Lastly, we have the attributes, which are essentially the information the object contains. These are usually also defined within the class, and this defines the object's state. Within the class of "cats," we can say that a domestic cat will be treated differently than a tiger. Their size could determine the state of the object and enable the software to define different reactions and actions for each type of cat.

## Concepts

- **Inheritance**: As you might imagine by the word, when we talk about inheritance in Java, we are talking about when an object inherits the properties and behavior of another object. This means that an object from a previous class can be passed on to another from a different class. However, I will not go into too much detail as we will see more of inheritance in the next chapter, Chapter 12.

- **Polymorphism**: If you analyze the word polymorphism, you will see that it means to assume multiple forms. Therefore, if you think about the concept within Java, you can consider that the language allows a different action to be performed in several different ways. This means that objects, variables, or functions can adopt different behaviors according to their requests. You might recognize this because polymorphism is directly related to method overloading, as we have seen in the previous chapter.

- **Abstraction**: When you have code that does not contain background information related to it. This means that you will only see what is necessary, and everything else will remain hidden. One of the advantages of using abstract classes and objects is that it will make your code more readable and organized. This approach is generally used when it is not necessary to see the inner workings of the code. Think about it as a watch: If you can correctly tell time, you don't need to think about how the mechanism works inside it.

- **Encapsulation**: When you think about a capsule, you probably imagine something inside a recipient to be protected or guarded against any outside interference. The same thing applies to this Java concept. Encapsulating the code means you are playing it within a single place to avoid other parts of the code from interfering with it. One of the encapsulation's main uses is declaring a class private instead of public. This way, all the information you want to maintain is contained inside a specific object containing all the relevant data pertaining to that block of code.

- **Association**: As the name might suggest, when you have an association in Java, it means that you are establishing a relationship between two classes by using an object or objects. If we go back to the cat example, you can think of it as the following: You can have a similar type of cat in several zoos or have one zoo with several of these cats. In addition, you can also have one zoo with one cat or many zoos with many cats. When you think about it from this perspective, you can see that there is no specific owner to this class of cats—each of them will be independent but common at the same time.

- **Aggregation**: Aggregation in Java is similar to an association, however, more limited. This means that every object you create will have its lifecycle but no owner (Hartman, 2019). For example, there can be many animals in a zoo, but there is no zoo if there are no animals. In this example, if we do not have a zoo, we will still have animals, but there is no utility for a zoo if there are no animals. In this case, the "child" object cannot belong to another "parent" object.

- **Composition**: The last concept is called composition, which is yet another type of association. In this case, the relationship will only be as long as the class exists. Once it ceases to do so, all the other objects will be deleted as well. Hartman (2019) calls it a "death" relationship because of this elimination characteristic where the objects do not have their lifecycle.

While I have not placed any examples of these concepts, you do not need to worry. As I mentioned, we will see more of each of them as we move on with the book. Therefore, hang on tight and keep reading.

## *Difference in Paradigm*

When I mentioned earlier that OOP is a programming paradigm, you might have asked yourself if there are others. To answer this question, I can say that there are others. When we talk about programming languages, we usually consider the three most common paradigms (although there are others): **functional programming**, **OOP**, and **procedural**

**programming**. These can be used in imperative programming, when a developer says exactly what the computer needs to do step-by-step, or in declarative programming, which is based on logic and *what* should be done rather than *how*.

To first understand a paradigm, we can define it as the way a program is organized or the language used when coding. When you consider each of these paradigms, we can say that depending on your choice will determine what your structure will look like and how you will solve problems. Cocca (2022) goes even further and says that each problem you face can have a better or worse solution depending on the paradigm you are using since not all languages are tied to a paradigm, or they can be associated with more than one.

- **Functional programming**: When we talk about functional programming, we are talking about a declarative form of programming. It will focus, much like mathematical functions, on what should be solved by using expressions and not statements. Some examples of functional programming languages include Scala, Python, and Racket.

- **Procedural programming**: Procedural programming is a form of imperative programming and will determine how the program should run from beginning to end according to the established steps. It contains variables just as much as a recipe would have. Therefore, when you think about procedural programming, you can think that it is like following a recipe you found in a cookbook that will give you the steps you need to take to make a specific dish. Some languages that use this paradigm are C, Pascal, and BASIC.

As you already know, OOP is an imperative form of programming based on objects, each with a specific task to make the code work. Other languages that use this programming method include Python and C++, apart from Java, of course. But, now the question is why OOP would be so much better or different from these other paradigms. Or, in other words, what are the benefits that make it one of the most popular paradigms in the market? Let's take a closer look at the benefits of having an OOP approach to the developer, the code, and the software you are building.

## The Benefits of OOP

If you were to speak to a developer who works with OOP and ask them about the benefits of using this approach to programming, they could probably give you a list of at least 10 reasons. It is safe to say that these professionals are very enthusiastic about using this form of development because some of its benefits include the possibility to reuse code, easy maintenance, security advantages, flexibility, and an easy way it facilitates problem-solving and troubleshooting.

Although the list is exhaustive, I could spend several pages of this book telling you all about its benefits and how you can apply OOP to almost any situation you wish to program. However, to make things concise, I will focus on three of the most important aspects of OOP that will help you understand better why it is one of the main approaches used by the market: **troubleshooting**, **productivity**, and **reusability**.

### *Troubleshooting*

When you are developing a program, you are likely dealing with hundreds of lines of code—this is usual, especially dealing with complex situations. When you have an OOP approach, troubleshooting these issues is easier because instead of having to look over everything you did, you can go directly to the object or class that is presenting the problem. If you consider that OOP brings to your code a concept of **modularity**, where the objects are self-contained, it also enables you to see the **encapsulation** concept in action.

Because of the encapsulation principle, where all the objects are constrained, if your program's response is unexpected, you will know exactly where the issue lies because the code is broken down into smaller parts, enabling you to tackle each one at a time. In addition to this, if you are using a compiler, it will indicate the exact position of the mistake or, in some cases, automatically fix it for you. This will save you time and make your coding more efficient.

### Increased Productivity

If you think about how you can use method overloading in Java and apply inheritance and polymorphism, you will understand why OOP allows the developer to have increased productivity. Considering that the same object can have different properties and be used in different manners by adapting its behavior, it will give the developer more flexibility and decrease the time they need to make a determined block of code to work.

There is also the advantage of having numerous available libraries that you can use to adapt your code. Additionally, you will have more readable code, facilitating the task of understanding, writing, and editing what you need. Last but not least, when using OOP, this makes your code highly scalable, enabling a small program to easily be expanded to a larger one if needed.

### Reusability

If when you think about code reusability, the first things that come to your mind are the concepts of polymorphism and inheritance, you are right on the spot! These two concepts enable classes and methods to be reused throughout the development process, saving the programmer's time.

When you have a code that you can reuse because you have applied inheritance properties to it, you don't need to keep rewriting it every time you need to apply the concept within the code. This gives the developer **flexibility** to work with the code. Therefore, when you create a class or a method that can be reused, you can apply it as many times as you need in your program while eliminating redundant lines of code.

### Criticism of OOP

Although there are many benefits to OOP, we could not end this section without speaking about some of the criticism that this programming paradigm has. It has been repeatedly criticized by developers because they believe OOP emphasizes too much the components of software development and not enough on computation or algorithms. In addition to this, others claim that when you have an OOP-based code, it can be more complicated due to its characteristics of attributing specific behaviors to each object. This makes it more demanding to write and takes longer to compile when needed.

**Getting Started With OOP in Java**

I have already gone over how you should create a method in the previous chapter, so now we will take a look at how to create a class and an object: essential parts of your Java programming. Take a look at the below code:

```java
public class Example {

public static void main(String[] args) {

int sum = 0;

for(int j = 1; j<=100; j++) {

sum = sum + j;

}

System.out.println("If you add all the numbers from 1 to 100 the answer is " + sum);

}

}
```

In this case, we have created a public class with the name Example. You will see that to create a class, you will need to use one of the modifiers (default, public, private, protected) associated with the word "class."

**Java convention**: The class should always start with a capital letter and, if it is composed of more than words, the beginning of each one should be capitalized. Another Java convention is that the name of the class should be the same as the file.

**Pro tip**: Java is case-sensitive, so remember to look at your methods, classes, and objects to ensure that they comply with the Java conventions I have mentioned.

The object will be according to the class that was declared, in this case, the variable declared was int sum = 0; and the object is for(int j = 1; j<=100; j++). You can create several objects within a class but also access an object from another class into the original class. As you might remember, this is the basic principle of inheritance. Let's look at another example:

public class Sample{

int a = 15;

public static void main(String[] args) {

Sample myObj = new Sample();

System.out.println(myObj.a);

}

}

The output will be 15. Here, note that we have created a class named Sample and we created an "int" variable with a value of 15. To create the new object, we associated it to a class in the following Sample myObj = new Sample();. Note that to create the new object, the word "new" was used in front of the name of the class.

Now, if we were to create a class with multiple objects, this is also possible. All you will need to do is repeat the step of creating the object. In this case, it would look like this:

public class Sample{//declared class

int a = 15;//declared variable

```
int b = 6;//declared variable
public static void main(String[] args) {//string that will store the line arguments
Sample myObj1 = new Sample();//creation of object 1
Sample myObj2 = new Sample();//creation of object 2
System.out.println(myObj1.a);
System.out.println(myObj2.b);
}
}
```

In this case, we have created two variables, a, which equals 15, and b, which equals 6. Therefore, when we run the program, the output will be 15 and 6. You could repeat the same object and, in this case, you would not need to create another variable, but just request that the print of **myObj1** and **myObj2** be variable "a." The result will then be for both outputs.

**Using Encapsulation to Improve Code Quality**

Although you already have an idea of what encapsulation is, let's take a deeper look at its meaning. When you use encapsulation, you are using one of the methods to recover and attribute value to the fields of an object. This way, when you need to perform an operation before attributing or calculating the value, you need to create **getters** and **setters** of the objects. You will also need to create the task examples that need to be performed in this code.

Although these elements were briefly discussed previously, you might be asking what getters and setters are. Hartman (2022) describes them as "two conventional methods used to retrieve and update values of a variable. They are mainly used to create, modify, delete, and view the variable values" (Getter and Setter in Java section). When we refer to the **setter** method, it means that we are updating values. On the other hand, when we mention **getter** methods, we are talking about reading the values. This means that depending on the type you decide to use, it is possible to only read or write the code.

Let's take a look at an example:

```
class Students{

private string student_name;

private int student_grade;

public int getName() { // getter method

return this.student_name;

}

public void setNumber(int num) { // setter method

this.student_grade = num;

}

}
```

In this example, the getName() method is, as the name suggests, a **getter that** will read the variable student_name. On the other hand, the **setter** method, characterized in setNumber(int num) will update the variable that refers to the student's grade. If we were to put it in a practical example, it would look like this:

```
public class Greeting{

private static String words;

public static String getWords(){

return words;

}

public void setWords(String words){

this.words=words;
```

144

```
}

public static void main(String[] args) {

Greeting yourObj = new Greeting();

yourObj.setWords("Hello, world");

System.out.println(yourObj.getWords());

}

}
```

As you can imagine, the output, in this case, will be "Hello, world."

# Implementing Polymorphism in Java and its Relation to Inheritance

Polymorphism in Java establishes that a method can be executed in different forms. Suppose you have the interface "geometric figure." When you have this situation, you are referring to all geometric figures, and you will implement methods that enable you to calculate their different areas. This means you will have the "square method," "circle method," "triangle method," and so on. This means that the class will still be the same, but the way each of the methods behaves is different because each geometric figure will be calculated distinctly.

Polymorphism is directly related to inheritance since it will enable the inheritance of the attributes and methods from another class. When you apply polymorphism to this, you are using these methods to perform different tasks, enabling you to do the same thing in different ways.

**Pro tip**: When you use the word "final" at the end of methods and classes, you are declaring that they cannot be reimplemented or extended. For example, all of those pertaining to the String method and even the String classes are considered final.

```java
class GeometricFigure{
public void shapeColor() {
System.out.println("The figure is");
}
}
class Square extends GeometricFigure {
public void shapeColor() {
System.out.println("The square is red");
}
}
class Circle extends GeometricFigure {
public void shapeColor() {
System.out.println("The circle is blue");
}
}
public class Main {
public static void main(String[] args) {
GeometricFigure mySquare = new Square(); // Create a Square object
GeometricFigure myCircle = new Circle(); // Create a Circle object
mySquare.shapeColor();
myCircle.shapeColor();
}
```

}

The output for this program will be:

The square is red

The circle is blue

As you will see, we have created two different shape colors, one for the square and red, and one for the circle and blue.

# Exercise

Now, I want you to try creating your own programs by using OOP.

1. Create a class Cat with characteristics of color, age, and weight, that purrs and meows.

**Solution**:

```
class Cat {
String color; //characteristic 1
int age; //characteristic 2
Double weight; //characteristic 3
public void purs() {//behavior 1 (method)
}
public void meows() {//behavior 2 (method)
}
}
```

2. Create a program that calculates the area of a circle and a triangle.

```
class GeometricFigure{
public void shapeArea() {
System.out.println("The area is");
}
}
class Circle extends GeometricFigure {
public void shapeArea() {
System.out.println("The circle area is 15.19");
```

```java
    }
}
class Triangle extends GeometricFigure {
    public void shapeArea() {
        System.out.println("The triangle area is 64");
    }
}
class Main {
    public static void main(String[] args) {
        GeometricFigure myCircle = new Circle();
        GeometricFigure myTriangle = new Triangle();
        myCircle.shapeArea();
        myTriangle.shapeArea();
    }
}
```

**Output**:

The circle area is 15.19

The triangle area is 64

# Summary

In this chapter, you have learned all about OOP, its characteristics and concepts, and the differences between programming paradigms.

You have also seen how the different concepts such as inheritance, polymorphism, and encapsulation benefit when you are coding in Java and how it makes the process more efficient.

Now, we will take a closer look at how to apply inheritance and another concept that we have briefly seen in this chapter: How to extend the Java language.

# Chapter 12: Application of Inheritance, Interface, and Extension in Java

Inheritance is a powerful tool in Java programming and for other languages that use OOP. Its main characteristic is that it allows you to extend the functionality of existing classes, meaning that it has a mechanism that enables an object to adopt the properties and behaviors of another class.

It's important to understand how inheritance works in Java so that you can take advantage of its benefits in your own programs. In this chapter, you will learn all about inheritance, interface, and extension in Java. While these are different concepts, you will soon see that they are closely related and that one needs the other to work correctly.

**Inheritance in Java**

Although inheritance is one of the advantages of using OOP, there is no one specific way to use it—there are several types of inheritance. JavaTpoint (n.d.-e) explains that when considering the old and the new class, you should remember the following:

> The existing (old) class is known as the **base class**, **superclass**, or **parent class**. The new class is known as a **derived class** or **subclass** or **child class**. It allows us to use the properties and behavior of one class (parent) in another class (child). (Inheritance section, para. 1)

To make sure that you indicate that these properties come from another class, you will use the word **extend**.

When you have a relationship between classes, it is also called an **Is-a relationship**. The concept of inheritance in Java is used for numerous reasons and one of the main ones is

**reusability and substitutability of the code**. These will allow the developer to shorten the number of lines they are applying and make the code more concise and readable.

When you have substitutability, this means that the child class will acquire the properties of the parent class and, thus, the object of the parent class can be substituted by the object of the child class. Suppose that B is a child class of A. This means that in any place where we can expect an instance of A, we can use an instance of B. This can be obtained by using inheritance by extensions or keyword implementation.

**Pro tip**: Although classes and methods can be reused, this is not true for constructors or private members. However, for a class to be reused, it cannot be given the **private** attribute.

*Types of Inheritance*

When we are speaking about inheritance in Java, most specialists consider five types that can be used (others consider four and some, even six) and this is the standard we will adopt for this book. They are: **single inheritance**, **multilevel inheritance**, **hierarchical inheritance**, **multiple inheritance**, and **hybrid inheritance**. Each of these types of inheritance has a characteristic and will be used for a different action you want to perform with your code. We will now see each of them in more detail with examples, to make comprehension easier.

To illustrate the example, we will use the following as our "classes":

- Chicago
- Illinois
- Arizona
- Texas
- United States

- North America

## Single Inheritance

Single inheritance happens when you have **one** class extending to another class. This means that only one child class will absorb the properties of the parent class. Our example would look like this:

public class NorthAmerica{

}

public class UnitedStates extends NorthAmerica{

}

In this case, the class **UnitedStates** will inherit the properties of the class **NorthAmerica**.

## Multilevel Inheritance

When you have a multilevel inheritance, the name already gives you a hint of what it does. This means you will have a parent class that will extend to a subclass and this subclass will become the parent class to another subclass. Our example would then look like this:

public class NorthAmerica{

}

public class UnitedStates extends NorthAmerica{

}

public class Chicago extends UnitedStates{

}

Here you have the same situation for the first two lines, but you can see that **Chicago** will extend from the UnitedSates parent class which, in turn, will be a child class of the parent class **NorthAmerica**.

## Hierarchical Inheritance

When we talk about hierarchical inheritance, this means that there is **one** parent class and several **child** classes. In our example, it would look like this:

```
public class UnitedStates{

}

public class Chicago extends United States{

}

public class Texas extends UnitedStates{

}

public class Arizona extends UnitedStates{

}
```

In this example, we have the parent class **UnitedStates** and three classes that extend from it: **Chicago**, **Texas**, and **Arizona**.

## Multiple Inheritance

What I am going to explain now might sound confusing but, although there is a multiple type of inheritance in Java, it does not work the same way as the others. The main reason for this is that you cannot have multiple inheritance if you are not using interfaces. **In Java, you are not able to use multiple inheritances with classes** and, therefore, you need to apply an interface to use it. This means that we could not extend **Chicago** to the parent classes **Arizona** and **Illinois**.

Since we have not seen the use of interfaces, I will not give you an example... yet. Further along in this chapter, I will speak about implementing interfaces with Java and then an example will be provided. For now, keep in mind that, **initially**, multiple inheritance is not allowed, but this can be changed when using interfaces.

**Hybrid Inheritance**

A hybrid interface happens in all classes when there is more than one type of inheritance in your code. However, as you have seen in the previous section, multiple inheritance, this is not possible without the use of interfaces. The same can be said for hybrid inheritance. This would mean that we would have, for example, **UnitedStates** extending to **Arizona** and **Illinois**, and **Arizona** and **Illinois** extending to **Chicago**. Since this means we would be applying a multiple inheritance, interfaces are, therefore, needed.

Just as with multiple inheritance, this will be approached further along in this chapter. For now, I want you to remember the concept to be used later. In the meantime, while we are not there yet, let's take a look at some of the benefits a developer will have by using inheritance in Java.

*Benefits of Using Inheritance*

To be able to reuse code that you have already created is one of the most relevant benefits of applying inheritance to your code. This means saving time and effort during development since the code won't need to be written again and again every time you need to use it. Another benefit is having a model structure that is easy to read and understand, as well as facilitating maintenance and saving up development costs (if you consider that less time will be spent coding).

When you use inheritance, you can override the class methods of the parent class to make implementation easier. Projecting the child class to the parent class also enables the developer to maintain the information as private, thus disabling the child class from making changes in the base class. However, there are also some disadvantages to using inheritance. Let's take a look at what they are.

## Disadvantages of Inheritance

When you have too many dependencies among the classes one of the main results is that your program will be slower to process. Think about it this way: The more one class depends on the other, the more time it will take the processor to analyze and compile everything because it needs to check that all references are correctly made. When you use large inheritance coding, you will demand more effort from the processor because all the classes are overcharged with dependencies.

You also need to remember that if you make a change in the parent class, you will need to alter the child class. If you have a simple inheritance, this could be an easy fix, but if you are using hierarchical inheritance, for example, depending on how many lines of code you need to change, this can prove to be a challenge.

The close relationship between the parent and the child classes will make them dependent on one another. If you think about it, when you use inheritance, if you do so incorrectly or excessively, it may lead to your program becoming more complex than necessary; thus, eliminating the benefits of readability and simplicity.

## Simple Example of Inheritance in Java

I imagine since you now know more about inheritance, you will see that one of the examples that we have previously used was exactly using inheritance. Remember when we were using the geometric figure example and we determined that the square was red and the circle was blue? Well, in this case, we associated two concepts that cannot exist without each other: inheritance and polymorphism. So that you do not need to go back, I have added the same example below for easier reference.

```
class GeometricFigure{

public void shapeColor() {

System.out.println("The figure is");
```

}

}

class Square extends GeometricFigure {//Square inherits from GeometricFigure

public void shapeColor() {

System.out.println("The square is red");

}

}

class Circle extends GeometricFigure {//Circle inherits from GeometricFigure

public void shapeColor() {

System.out.println("The circle is blue");

}

}

public class Main {

public static void main(String[] args) {

GeometricFigure mySquare = new Square();

GeometricFigure myCircle = new Circle();

mySquare.shapeColor();

myCircle.shapeColor();

}

}

In this case, GeometricFigure is the superclass of the Square and the Circle classes. As you can see in the comments, both of these new classes are inheriting their characteristics from the GeometricFigure superclass. Do you think you can identify what type of inheritance was used here? If you guessed **hierarchical inheritance**, you are correct! If you guessed it wrong, I suggest going back to the explanation of Java types and reviewing the information before you move on to the next section of this chapter.

**Creating a Parent Class**

To create a base class in Java, you will do it as you would with any other class. You will first need to give it a name and determine its fields, constructors, and methods. All this together will establish the creation of the parent or base class. Let's look at an example.

```java
public class UnitedStates{//parent class

public int population;// field 1

public int area;//field 2

public UnitedStates(int population, int area)//constructor

{

this.population = population;

this.area = area;

}

public void numberBirths(int increment) //method

{

population += increment;

}

public String toString() //

{

return ("The population is: " + this.population + "\n area is: " + this.area);

}
```

}

## Creating a Child Class

Next, we will need to create the child, or derived class. You will do this by calling the previous class. Let's take a look:

public class Illinois extends UnitedStates {

public int cities;//when you add this class, you will need to add another field

public Illinois(int population, int area, int cities)

{

super(population, area);//here we involve the UnitedStates constructor

this.cities = cities;

}

public void setDiscticts(int newDistribution)//add another method for this class

{

cities = newDistribution;

}

@Override public String toString()

{

return (super.toString() + "\ncities: "+ cities);

}

}

## Writing a Main Method to Use Both Classes

Now, we will need to create a main method to execute the code.

public class Main

{

public static void main (String[] argos)

```
{
Illinois st = new Illinois (1267, 150, 1456);
System.out.println(st.toString());
}
}
```

Your code is now ready. All you will need to do is place everything together in the IDE to make sure that the information you want will come out. Try it out! The output should be:

**The population is**: **1267**

**area is**: **150**

**Cities**: **1456**

*So, did you get it right?*

***How to Write a Main Method to Instantiate and Use Objects From Both Classes***

**Parent Class**:

```
public class AirCraft { //Parent Class
public AirCraft(String fuel, String engine) { // Constructor
this.fuel = fuel;
this.engine = engine;
}
private String fuel; //fields Parent Class
private String engine; //fields Parent Class
public String getFuel() { //method Parent Class
return fuel;
}
```

```java
public void setFuel(String fuel) { //method Parent Class
this.fuel = fuel;
}
public String getEngine() { //method Parent Class
return engine;
}
public void setEngine(String engine) {//method Parent Class
this.engine = engine;
}
@Override
public String toString() {//method
return "AirCraft{" +
"fuel='" + fuel + '\'' +//will print the slash
", engine='" + engine + '\'' +//will print the slash
'}'; //supposed to print the key image, which is why it is with single quote marks
}
}
```

**Child Class**:

```java
public class Drone extends AirCraft { // Subclass
private int pilots; //field Subclass
public Drone(String fuel, String engine, int pilots) { // Constructor Subclass
super(fuel, engine);
this.pilots = pilots;
}
public int getPilots() { // Method Subclass
```

```java
    return pilots;
}
public void setPilots(int pilots) { // Method Subclass
    this.pilots = pilots;
}
@Override
public String toString() { // Method Subclass
    return "Drone{" +
    "fuel='" + super.getFuel() + '\'' +
    ", engine='" + super.getEngine() + '\''
    + "pilots=" + pilots +
    '}';
    }
}
```

**Executor**

```java
public class Executor {
public static void main(String[] args) { // method main
AirCraft airCraft = new AirCraft("GAS", "rocket"); // Instantiating Parent Class
Drone drone = new Drone("electric", "propellers", 0); // Instantiating subclass
System.out.println(airCraft.toString()); //Calling Parent Class method
System.out.println(drone.toString()); //Calling Subclass method
}
}
```

The output for this case will be:

AirCraft{fuel='GAS', engine='rocket'}

Drone{fuel='electric', engine='propellers'pilots=0}

## Instantiating Objects From the Base Class

Based on the code block we used in the previous example, to instantiating object from the base class is done in the following line:

```
AirCraft airCraft = new AirCraft("GAS", "rocket"); // Instantiating base class
```

## Instantiating Objects From the Derived Class

On the other hand, still using the previous example, to instantiate the object from the derived class, the following code is used:

```
Drone drone = new Drone("electric", "propellers", 0); // Instantiating subclass
```

## Using Methods From Both Classes

When we want to use methods from both classes, this can also be seen in the above example. The part of the code that refers to this is:

```
System.out.println(airCraft.toString()); //calling base class method
```

```
System.out.println(drone.toString()); //Calling subclass method
```

Now it is your turn! In the following section, I will propose a few situations and will ask you to develop the code accordingly. The solution will be right below so you can check your work after you are done.

### *Exercise*

1. Create a base class named "mobile" with number and carrier properties.
2. Create a derived class called "landline" with the property address.
3. Write a main method to instantiate and use objects from both classes. Create an object for each and print all the properties of each object.

### Answer

1. *Create a base class named "mobile" with number and carrier properties.*

```
public class Mobile {

private String number;
```

```java
private String carrier;

public Mobile(String number, String carrier) {

this.number = number;

this.carrier = carrier;

}

public String getNumber() {

return number;

}

public void setNumber(String number) {

this.number = number;

}

public String getCarrier() {

return carrier;

}

public void setCarrier(String carrier) {

this.carrier = carrier;

}

}
```

2. *Create a derived class called "landline" with the property address.*

```java
public class LandLine extends Mobile{

public LandLine(String number, String carrier, String address) {

super(number, carrier);

this.address = address;

}

private String address;
```

```java
public String getAddress() {
return address;
}
public void setAddress(String address) {
this.address = address;
}
}
```

3. *Write a main method to instantiate and use objects from both classes. Create an object for each and print all the properties of each object.*

```java
public class Executor {
public static void main(String[] args) { // method main
Mobile mobile = new Mobile("+1 (123) 1234567", "Telecom A");
LandLine landLine = new LandLine("+1 (123) 1234567", "Telecom B", "5th, Avenue");
System.out.println(
"Mobile [number:" + mobile.getNumber() + ", carrier:" + mobile.getCarrier() + "]");
System.out.println(
"Landline [number:" + landLine.getNumber() + ", carrier:" + landLine.getCarrier() + ", address:" + landLine.getAddress() + "]");
}
}
```

**The output should be**:

Mobile [number:+1 (123) 1234567, carrier:Telecom A]

Landline [number:+1 (123) 1234567, carrier:Telecom B, address:5th, Avenue]

Now that you have learned and practiced inheritance, it is time to take a look at the first of the related issues to it: interfaces. As I explained at the beginning of the chapter, interfaces will be essential to code using multiple and hybrid inheritances. The next section of this chapter will teach you more about what these interfaces are, how they can be used, and when and why they should be used.

# Using Interfaces With Java

Interfaces are a way of specifying what a class can do without having to specify how it does it. This is especially useful in Java programming where many classes can implement the same interface. By knowing how to work with interfaces, you can make your code more flexible and easier to work. In addition to this, once you learn how to use interfaces, you will be able to apply multiple and hybrid inheritance, making your code even more efficient.

## *What Are Interfaces?*

While you read about **interfaces**, you will see that it is very similar to what classes are and how they work in Java. However, an interface is considered **abstract** because it does not specify how the class acts. In other words, the interfaces will determine the *what* but not the *how* of a specific class.

Interfaces are applied by using keywords. "In general terms, an interface can be defined as a container that stores the signatures of the methods to be implemented in the code segment. It improves the levels of Abstraction" (Ravikiran A S, 2022a, What is Interface in Java section). When you apply interfaces to your code, you will see that it will make it easier and more flexible to work with.

It will have method signatures, fields, and default methods, the last one being added to the Java 8 version. According to Ojha (2021), these changes were needed due to the previous limitations that coding in Java presented, thus taking the language creators to make the modifications.

> Before Java 8, interfaces could have only abstract methods. The implementation of these methods has to be provided in a separate class. So, if a new method is to

be added to an interface, then its implementation code has to be provided in the class implementing the same interface. To overcome this issue, Java 8 has introduced the concept of default methods which allow the interfaces to have methods with implementation without affecting the classes that implement the interface. (Ojha, 2021, para. 1)

But if they are so similar to classes, how does one compare with interfaces? What are the differences in syntax and how does the abstract method come in? To make your understanding clearer, here is a table that compares interfaces and classes, provided by Ravikiran A S (2022a, Interface vs Class section):

| Interface | Class |
| --- | --- |
| Keyword used: **interface** | Keyword used: **class** |
| Does not have a constructor | Includes a constructor |
| Stores only the signature of a method | Stores complete method definition |
| Does not need access specifiers | Access specifiers are mandatory |
| Does not include data members | Includes data members |
| Does not have static members | Includes static members |

Now that you understand some of the basic differences, we will now see how we can work with interfaces and apply them to our code.

## How to Work With Interfaces

To start off, you need to know that to use an interface, the class must first implement it. This means that the class has to provide an implementation for all the methods in the interface. Once the class has implemented the interface, it can be used anywhere that the interface is used.

In the following example, you will see the coding example of an interface:

```
public interface Animal{//declaration of class
public String Name = "";//field
public void age();//method 1
public void weight();//method 2
default void meow(){//default method
System.out.println("Cat meows");
}
}
```

Although on its own it will not mean much for the program you are developing when you associate it with a class, you will see that it makes more sense. Suppose that we add the following to this code:

```
public class Cat implements Animal{
public void age() {
System.out.println("Age is");
}
public void weight() {
System.out.println("The weight is");
```

}

}

**Pro tip**: When you are using interfaces, always ensure that the class implements all the methods in the interface with the same name that was described. The fields do not need to be declared (FreeCodeCamp, 2020). In addition to this, when you create an interface, you can't add a constructor method to it, thus disabling the possibility of creating an instance of the interface itself.

As you might have seen in the previous code example, to apply a default method, we added to the code the word **default**. When you use this expression in your code, it will enable you to use expressions without having to implement the methods in the classes. When you do this, the implementation will automatically be available and we won't need to change the rest of the code, preserving compatibility. This will make it easier to apply polymorphism and inheritance to your code since it will be possible to add several interfaces to the same block of code.

**Pro tip**: All of the members of a default interface are considered public, thus not needing to declare **public** in the statement.

### The Disadvantage of Interfaces

When you have a Java program, there are two approaches to using interfaces: either the developer uses it extensively or they do not use it at all. One of the reasons that some developers avoid using it is because applying it can reduce the execution time of a program. If you associate the delayed execution time of using inheritance *plus* the execution time that it takes a program to run when using interfaces, you might have a program that takes too long to respond.

## Why Use Interfaces?

When thinking about the reasons to use interfaces, the one that stands out is that it will make the classes in your code adopt behaviors that are not native to them, creating more flexible and dynamic code. Since when implementing interfaces you will only determine what the class will do, it will be easier to maintain and understand what you have written because multiple inheritance will be able to be modeled within the structure. If your case is that you want to achieve full abstraction in your code, then it is also possible by implementing interfaces, as you will now see.

### Abstract Classes and Interfaces

In Java, when there is an abstraction, it means that you are hiding a part of the code. In this case, you would be showing the user only the part of the code that they need to see since they are not essential to them. You can apply the concept of abstract to classes or interfaces, which will allow the focus of the code to be on what the object will do instead of *how*.

To apply abstraction to your code, you will need to use the **abstract** keyword. It can be applied to classes, methods, and constructors. However, you need to keep in mind that when you have an abstract class, this does not necessarily mean that you will have an abstract method. In this case, you can use an abstract class with a normal method. In an example of a syntax using abstraction, the code would look like this:

*For a class:*

abstract class Example{}

*For a method:*

abstract void printExample();

*Example of abstract class, abstract method, and public method:*

abstract class Dog{

```java
public abstract voiddogSound();

public void excited() {

System.out.println("Woof! Woof!");

}

}
```

*Code complete with abstract class, method, constructor, and data member:*

```java
abstract class Boat{ //declare abstract class

Boat(){System.out.println("Boat navigates");} //declare method

abstract void navigate(); //declare abstract method

void changeOrientation(){System.out.println("Orientation changed");}

}

class Yacht extends Boat{ //inheritance from an abstract class

void navigate(){System.out.println("Navigating on course");}

}

public class Test{ //calls abstract and non-abstract methods

public static void main(String args[]){ //calling Main method

Boat obj = new Yacht(); //create object

obj.navigate(); //calling method declared in boat class and implemented in yacht

obj.changeOrientation(); //calling method implemented in abstract class

}

}
```

**The output will be**:

Boat navigates

171

Navigating on course

Orientation changed

Now you already know how to use abstract in your code, be it with interfaces or with classes. However, since one of the main objectives of interfaces is to enable the creation of multiple and hybrid inheritance, let's take a look at two examples where this is used.

**Using Interfaces to Create Multiple Inheritance**

For this example, I have placed the explanation of the code in comment format within the syntaxes for better understanding.

```java
public interface Vehicle {//application of interface in class

String move();//declaration of method signature in the interface

}

public interface Personal {//application of interface in class

int numberOfWheels();//declaration of method signature in the interface

int numberOfPassengers();//declaration of method signature in the interface

}

public class Bicycle implements Personal, Vehicle{//inheritance using implement

@Override

public int numberOfWheels() {//implementation of declared method in interface

return 2;

}

@Override

public int numberOfPassengers() {//implementation of declared method in interface
```

```java
return 1;

}

@Override

public String move() {//implementation of declared method in interface

return "Starting to pedal...";

}

}

public class Executor {//declaration of public class

public static void main(String[] args) {//declaration of Main method

Bicycle bicycle = new Bicycle();//object creation

System.out.println("To move a Bicycle you need: [" + bicycle.move() + "]");

System.out.println("Bicycle has Space for: [" + bicycle.numberOfPassengers() + "] passengers");

System.out.println("Bicycle has : [" + bicycle.numberOfWheels() + "] wheels");

}

}
```

The output will be:

To move a Bicycle you need: [Starting to pedal...]

Bicycle has Space for: [1] passengers

Bicycle has: [2] wheels

In this case, you will see that we have used two parent classes using inheritance to call out the bicycle. Without using **interface** for both personal and vehicle, this would not be possible.

**Using Interfaces to Create Hybrid Inheritance**

The following example will show you how interfaces can be used to create hybrid inheritance. Similar to the previous example, I will add the comments with the explanation next to each line of code for better understanding and clarity.

```
public interface Vehicle {//application of interface as a class

String move();//declaration of method signature in the interface

}

public class Car extends Motorized implements Vehicle{

@Override

public String move() {

return "Starting motor type: ["+getMotor()+"]";

}

}

public class ExecutorCar {

public static void main(String[] args) {//calling out Main method to execute code

Car car = new Car();//create object

car.setMotor("V8");

System.out.println("To move a car you need: [" + car.move() + "]");

}

}
```

The output for this example will be:

To move a car you need: [Starting motor type: [V8]]

Now that you have seen the application of Java by using interfaces, it is your turn to test what you have learned. In this next section, I will propose two exercises for you to practice and see if you have correctly understood the concepts presented in this section.

### Exercise

1. You are creating an application to manage vehicles and want to represent their different types (cars, motorcycles, boats, etc.) using classes and interfaces. What would this code look like? For this example, the output should be:

   Car moving.

   Car engine started.

   Boat moving.

   Boat navigating.

**Answer possibility**:

```java
public interface Vehicle {
    void move();
}
public interface Motorized {
    void startEngine();
}
public interface Navigable {
    void navigate();
}
public class Car implements Vehicle, Motorized {
    public void move() {
        System.out.println("Car moving.");
```

```java
    }
    public void startEngine() {
        System.out.println("Car engine started.");
    }
}
public class Boat implements Vehicle, Navigable {
    public void move() {
        System.out.println("Boat moving.");
    }
    public void navigate() {
        System.out.println("Boat navigating.");
    }
}
public class Executor {
    public static void main(String[] args) {
        Car car = new Car();
        Boat boat = new Boat();
        car.move();
        car.startEngine();
        boat.move();
        boat.navigate();
    }
}
```

2. You are creating a game and you want to represent the different types of players (human players and bots) using classes and interfaces. What would your code look like? The output in this case should be:

Human player playing.

Human player controlling.

Computer player playing.

**Answer possibility**:

```java
public interface Player {
void play();
}
public interface Controllable {
void control();
}
public class Computer implements Player {
public void play() {
System.out.println("Computer player playing.");
}
}
public class Human implements Player, Controllable {
public void play() {
System.out.println("Human player playing.");
}
public void control() {
System.out.println("Human player controlling.");
}
```

```java
}
public class Executor {
public static void main(String[] args) {
Human human = new Human();
Computer computer = new Computer();
human.play();
human.control();
computer.play();
}
}
```

# Extending the Java Language

Extending the Java language is a powerful way to add new functionality to existing code. By understanding the basics of how to extend the language, you can make your code more flexible and robust. "Extensions add new functionality to an existing class, structure, enumeration, or protocol type. This includes the ability to extend types for which you don't have access to the original source code" (Swift, n.d., para. 1).

### *Basic Concepts of Extending the Java Language*

When we use the word **extends** in Java, we are basically saying that it is inheriting the properties from the class which it is calling. As we have seen in previous examples, the syntax would be as simple as class B extends A. This would mean that we have previously declared parent class A and that child class B is absorbing its properties.

However, here it is important to note that when you use extend, it can only extend one class. You might think that this is very similar to implementation and, in fact, it is. To eliminate any doubts you might have regarding both concepts, here is a table provided by Gauravmoney26 (2020) that highlights the main differences between both (para. 7):

| Extends | Implements |
|---|---|
| *Regarding classes*: a class can inherit another class, or an interface can inherit other interfaces. | *Regarding classes*: A class can implement an interface. |
| It is not compulsory that a subclass that extends a superclass override all the methods in a superclass. | It is compulsory that a class implementing an interface has to implement all the methods of that interface. |
| Only one superclass can be extended by a class. | A class can implement any number of interfaces at a time. |
| Any number of interfaces can be extended by interface. | An interface can never implement any other interface. |

## Why Extend the Java Language?

You will want to use the extend keyword when you want to apply inheritance characteristics to your code. It will be especially useful to make the child class absorb the properties and behavior of the parent class. Additionally, when you use extend, you are clearly stating that there is a relationship between both classes. If you consider that this principle is directly related to the inheritance concept, you will conclude that you will implement it for the same reasons you would inheritance in general: to make your code easier and more manageable.

## How to Extend the Java Language

To extend your Java code, all you will need to do is to add the **extend** keyword to the syntax after you have declared a parent class. We have already seen many examples of this application throughout the book, although the concept is only being explained now. To see an example of the use of extend, we can use the following example:

```java
class GeometricFigure{//parent class declared

public void shapeColor() {

System.out.println("The figure is");

}

}

class Square extends GeometricFigure {//declare child class that extends from parent

public void shapeColor() {//absorbs the characteristics in the method

System.out.println("The square is red");

}

}

class Circle extends GeometricFigure {//declare child class that extends from parent

public void shapeColor() {//absorbs the characteristic in the method

System.out.println("The circle is blue");

}

}

public class Main {

public static void main(String[] args) {

GeometricFigure mySquare = new Square(); // Create a Square object

GeometricFigure myCircle = new Circle(); // Create a Circle object

mySquare.shapeColor();

myCircle.shapeColor();
```

}

}

The output for this program will be:

The square is red

The circle is blue

As you have seen in this example, we created a parent class called GeometricFigure that had a method associated with it under the name shapeColor(). Since we were going to use the characteristic of this method for the object "square" and the object "circle," we applied inheritance to avoid repeating the code and applying the method to both new classes at once, in this case, class Circle and class Square, both of which were extended from GeometricFigure.

**Basic Concepts of Extension**

When we think about an extension, there are two concepts we need to think about that were not previously approached in the book and will be essential to understand. The first is the use of the keyword **final** and the second refers to **inner classes.**

**Using Final**

When you add the keyword **final** to a method or a class, this means it cannot be extended. Suppose we use the previous example and add final to the syntax like this:

public final class GeometricFigure{

Public final void shapeColor() {

System.out.println("The figure is");

}

}

If you did this when you tried to run class Circle and class Square, it would give you a compilation error because it can't be extended. Therefore, adding final to your code is declaring the "death" of a class. Now, you might be asking, *Why would I add "final" to my code? In what ways would I benefit from this?* Well, it just so happens that when you add this keyword to your code, it also makes it unchangeable when an object is created.

I want you to try an example. Get the code I have given you from the previous example for class Circle and class Square. Place it on your IDE and run it. You should have the previously mentioned output. Now, go back and add final, as we did above to this code and try running it again. You will see that the IDE will give you back an error that will look like this:

/Main.java:6: error: **cannot inherit from final GeometricFigure**

class Square extends GeometricFigure {//declare child class that extends from parent

^

/Main.java:11: error: **cannot inherit from final GeometricFigure**

class Circle extends GeometricFigure {//declare child class that extends from parent

As you can see, the compiler itself is already giving you the answer on what is wrong with the code. We will learn more about errors and how to fix them in Chapter 14.

**Using Inner Classes**

In Java, when you use an **inner class**, this means that you are going to declare it, as the name suggests, inside the class or interface you are going to use. This idea of grouping classes in one place in the code is a technique commonly used to make the code reader-friendly and make it easier to identify where each piece of information is.

According to JavaTpoint (2011), one of the advantages of using inner classes is that they will enable you to access members in both the inner and the outer classes, including private data and methods. When you apply the logic of these inner classes to your developing process, you are also using another tactic which is to hide the information within other classes.

**Pro tip**: When we use the code in a compiler or an IDE, it generally automatically indents the code for you. This way, it will be easier to understand what is within what and how each part of the code relates to the others. Although there is no specific declaration of an inner class, once you add them in the IDE, you will see that they are indented within the class where they are contained, thus characterizing them as inner or nested classes.

## Applying the Concepts of Extending the Java Language

If you have understood the concepts that were presented so far to you in this chapter, it is likely that you will not have a hard time understanding the extension. The main thing here is that the general idea of inheritance application is clear, as well as the differences of when to add interfaces and when to add extend.

If you still have doubts, I recommend going back to the beginning of the chapter and writing the code examples in your IDE to understand how they work. Additionally, you should try creating some of your own codes to ensure that the concepts were correctly understood. Do as many examples as you need until you feel confident about what has been explained.

In this section, we will take a look at some examples of how to use the **extends** keyword in your code. We will also see how they can be used with abstract classes and the **final** keyword, also two concepts that we have approached. Read the examples below and clarify any doubts you might have.

### How to Extend the Java Language Using Interfaces

If you are thinking that we have already seen how to extend Java by using interfaces, you are correct! When I spoke about the application of interfaces in your code, all the examples where the word **interface** appears, it is already an example of its application. To refresh your memory and look at a quick example, see the below syntax:

```
public interface Player {

void play();
```

}

This is an example of Java language extension using interfaces.

### How to Extend the Java Language Using Abstract Classes

In the following example, we have a gaming scenario. Here, suppose the **Player** interface represents the ability to play, and the **Controllable** interface represents the ability to be controlled. You will need to create an abstract class named **AbstractPlayer** that will implement the **Player** interface and provide a way to store their name.

The **HumanPlayer** class will extend from **AbstractPlayer** and implement the **Controllable** interface, providing specific implementations for the methods declared in them. At the same time, the **ComputerPlayer** class extends from **AbstractPlayer** and only implements the **Player** interface, indicating that it can play but it is not controllable.

```java
public interface Player {

void play();

}

public interface Controllable {

void control();

}

public abstract class AbstractPlayer implements Player {

protected String name;

public AbstractPlayer(String name) {

this.name = name;

}

}
```

```java
public class ComputerPlayer extends AbstractPlayer {
public ComputerPlayer(String name) {
super(name);
}
public void play() {
System.out.println(name + " is playing.");
}
}
public class HumanPlayer extends AbstractPlayer implements Controllable {
public HumanPlayer(String name) {
super(name);
}
public void play() {
System.out.println(name + " is playing.");
}
public void control() {
System.out.println(name + " is controlling.");
}
}
public class Executor {
public static void main(String[] args) {
HumanPlayer human = new HumanPlayer("Abott");
ComputerPlayer computerPlayer = new ComputerPlayer("Hal");
human.play();
human.control();
```

```
computerPlayer.play();

}

}
```

The output should be:

Abott is playing.

Abott is controlling.

Hal is playing.

By programming this way, you can use the properties and methods of the abstract class in all classes that extend it, creating an instance of a player without knowing if it is a human or a computer player.

***How to Extend the Java Language Using Inner Classes***

In this example, we have a different situation than the previous example. Here, the program defines an interface called **Player**, which has a single method play(). The **Game** class has a private field named **gameName** and a constructor that sets the value of the **gameName** field. The **Game** class also defines two inner classes from **AbstractPlayer** called **HumanPlayer** and **ComputerPlayer**.

In this case, the **AbstractPlayer** implements the **Player** interface and has a protected field name and a constructor that sets the value of the name field. **HumanPlayer** and **ComputerPlayer** classes are inner classes and both of them extend **AbstractPlayer**. This means they will inherit the name field and the constructor. Both classes have their own implementation of the **play()** method, which is defined in the **Player** interface.

```
interface Player {
void play();
}
```

```java
public class Game {
private String gameName;
public Game(String gameName) {
this.gameName = gameName;
}
abstract class AbstractPlayer implements Player {
protected String name;
public AbstractPlayer(String name) {
this.name = name;
}
}
class HumanPlayer extends AbstractPlayer {
public HumanPlayer(String name) {
super(name);
}
public void play() {
System.out.println(name + " is playing " + gameName + ".");
}
}
class ComputerPlayer extends AbstractPlayer {
public ComputerPlayer(String name) {
super(name);
}
public void play() {
System.out.println(name + " is playing " + gameName + ".");
```

```
}
}
public static void main(String[] args) {
Game game = new Game("chess");
Game.HumanPlayer humanPlayer = game.new HumanPlayer("John");
humanPlayer.play();
Game.ComputerPlayer computerPlayer = game.new ComputerPlayer("AI");
computerPlayer.play();
}
}
```

The output will be:

John is playing chess.

AI is playing chess.

As you can see in the code for this example, the play() method printed a message that includes the name of the player and the name of the game, and the main method created an instance of the Game class and sets the value of the gameName field to "Chess." It then created an instance of the HumanPlayer class, setting the name field to "John" and calling the play() method on it. Finally, it also creates an instance of the ComputerPlayer class, setting the name field to "AI" and calling the play() method on it.

**How to Extend the Java Language Using Inheritance**

If you remember our inheritance section, you will see that most of the examples we have used for extension were already using inheritance. You can identify this by the syntax here:

```
public interface Player {
```

```java
void play();
}

public interface Controllable {
void control();
}

public abstract class AbstractPlayer implements Player {//inheritance from Player
protected String name;
public AbstractPlayer(String name) {
this.name = name;
}
}

public class ComputerPlayer extends AbstractPlayer {//inheritance from AbstractPlayer
public ComputerPlayer(String name) {
}
```

# Summary

In this chapter, you have learned all the information necessary to use inheritance, interfaces, and extension in your Java code. These are tools and concepts that will make your coding easier and enable you to create a cleaner visual for your code. You now understand the different types of inheritance a Java code can have and how to apply each of them when you are programming.

However, remember to apply them with precaution—using too much inheritance, extensions, and interfaces will make your compilation take more time and make your program slower.

Once again, I would like to suggest you take some time with this chapter which is very content-heavy to practice the concepts you have learned so far. Use the examples I have given you, adapt them, and create your own exercises. Since you have the outputs, it should be easy.

I also want to encourage you to continue even if there is a mistake in your code—it is through these that we will learn what is being done wrong and where we can improve. If you have encountered an error, try fixing it by using the tips that are provided in the compiler output box.

If even after you have tried you still can't find a solution, don't worry.

In the next chapter, we will take a look at Java collections to finalize the last part of important basic concepts and we will move on to common errors and debugging. Therefore, hold on to this mistake so that you can learn from it when we get there.

Now, off we go to learn more about collections and frameworks in Java.

# Chapter 13: Creating and Using Collections in Java

The Java collections framework is a set of classes and interfaces that provide a standard way of working with different types of data structures. The framework is one of the core characteristics of Java and is used by developers all over the world to make their work easier and more efficient. With so many different data structures available, the Java collections framework is an essential tool for any Java programmer. According to Ravikiran A S (2022b):

> Java Collections are the one-stop solutions for all the data manipulation jobs such as storing, searching, sorting, inserting, deletion, and updating of data. Java collection responds as a single object, and a Java Collection Framework provides various Interfaces and Classes. (para. 1)

**The Java Collections Framework**

The Java collections framework is a set of classes and interfaces that implement commonly used data structures. It also serves as a way to group distinct items in one place, helping you to keep your code organized. When you use the Java collection framework, it allows you to group both frameworks and interfaces, allowing different types of data structures to be used in the same program.

It also provides you with a standard way of handling data structures and program efficiency. When you think about collections, you will need to remember that they are composed of interfaces, implementations, and algorithms (Tutorials Point, n.d.-e).

In the interface collections and classes, we will have the following options:

- **Iterator interfaces**: These are possible to be implemented in all classes and interfaces and, therefore, considered the general interfaces for Java. "The primary function of an iterator is to allow the user to traverse through all of the collection class objects as if they were simple sequences of data items" (Kirloskar, 2021, Iterable section).

- **Collection interfaces**: Used to establish hierarchy and prove the facility to use all other collections. An important detail is that it only has a method signature. It roots down from the iterable interfaces and will be the start where all the other interfaces will branch out from.

- **List interface**: As the name might suggest, a list interface orders elements. It expands from the collection interface and is one of the most used interfaces in the Java collection. It expands to array list, linked list, and vector.

    - **ArrayList class**: As we have seen in Chapter 7, the array list is very commonly used in Java to organize information. When you are implementing an array, you can apply all the list methods and all elements can be null and unsynchronized. For more examples of how to use the array list, go back to the relevant chapter where you will learn all the necessary information on how to use it.

    - **LinkedList class**: A linked list can be described as a Java structure that is linear in which the elements, different from an array, are not stored in fixed positions. This means that the next element on the list will be linked to the previous one, which will be its reference or address.

    - **Vector class:** When you apply the vector interface, you are using a form of array that is more dynamic, since they are synchronized. For other functionalities, they will use the same as those in the ArrayList class.

- **Queue interface**: The second interface that expands the collection interface is known as the queue. Its main characteristic, if you imagine a queue, is that it is used by order, something like a first-in-first-out (FIFO) structure. The only exception to this rule is when the PriorityQueue class is implemented, which we will see in a little bit.

- **Deque class**: In the first expandable class from the queue interface, the deque class is composed of a linear structure that has two ends. This means that you can either insert or delete in either spot of the queue and will establish the element that will be used first by being the last or the first.

- **PriorityQueue class**: This is for when a list is established according to a specific order and establishing priorities. An additional characteristic is that elements contained within it will be ordered according to their natural sequence unless determined to the contrary.

- **Set interface**: The set is the third interface that branches out from the collection interface. One of its main characteristics is that there cannot be double elements within it. It is also a mathematical definition of a set representing a collection of objects with a maximum of one null element.

    - **HashSet class**: This class is one of the two that implements the Set interface, with the other being the LinkedHas Set. When you use this class, you are also creating a HashCode and an algorithm that will distribute the elements in the set. It does not establish an order between the elements, although it does permit an element to be null. When you create a HashSet, each element will be directed to its relevant bucket (Kirloskas, 2021).

    - **LinkedHashSet class**: You can consider the LinkedHashSet class to be the same as the HashSet class, with the difference that all the buckets it will use have a double list.

    - **SortedSet class**: As the name suggests, the SortedSet class will enable you to sort the data according to your preferences.

    - **TreeSet class**: To understand the TreeSet class, you will need to use the real-world representation of its name: a tree. When you think about one, you will see that it grows in a specific order, and that there is a sequence to it. The same will happen in the TreeSet class, where the elements are always placed in their natural order in an unsynchronized way.

Last but not least, we will have a separate interface group named **Map**. It is extended by other implementations and will enable you to assign a value to certain keys. The three types of implementations are the HashMap, the TreeMap, and the LinkedHashMap. As you might have noticed, these have similar names to the classes and interfaces because they act similarly, with the difference of the key attribution to each of the elements in the list.

**Common Operations on Collections**

Several common operations can be performed on collections. Das (2022) lists 10 common uses for collection in Java as follows:

1. Checking if a collection is empty
2. Getting the size of a collection
3. Checking if an element is in a collection
4. Adding an element to a collection
5. Removing an element from a collection
6. Iterating over a collection
7. Sorting a collection
8. Searching a collection
9. Checking if two collections are equal
10. Printing a collection

As you might imagine from what these collections do, some of them use logical operations, such as "OR" and "AND," and others use no-logical approaches. This will enable the developer to reduce the time it takes to develop a code and present a program with more quality.

## Creating and Using Collections

There are many ways to create and use collections in Java. Some of the most common ways to create and use collections include creating an ArrayList, a HashMap, adding elements to a collection, iterating a collection, and removing elements from a collection. Although there are several other possibilities, I have selected the most used applications to exemplify.

**Pro tip**: To use a collection, you will need to indicate where it is located within the Java core library. You will need to state which library they are located in; therefore, you will need to import a concept that we have seen in Chapter 1 when we were creating our first code. To create a HashMap, for example, you would need to import the import java.util.HashMap library and this will need to be placed at the beginning of your code. It is important to note here that if you do not import these libraries the code will not follow as expected and an error will show once you compile.

### Creating an ArrayList

An ArrayList is a data structure that is backed by an array. They are often used because they are easy to use, flexible, dynamic, and efficient. An example of an ArrayList would be:

```
import java.util.ArrayList;//import the correct class
import java.util.List;//import the correct interface
public class ArrayExample {
public static void main(String[] args) {
```

```java
List<String> fruits = new ArrayList<>();//start array list here
fruits.add("Apple");//list item 1
fruits.add("Banana");//list item 2
fruits.add("Orange");//list item 3
fruits.add("Mango");//list item 4
fruits.add("Pineapple");//list item 5
System.out.println("Iterating using for loop:");
for (int i = 0; i < fruits.size(); i++) {
System.out.println(fruits.get(i));
}
}
}
```

As you can see, we created an ArrayList with five items: apple, banana, orange, mango, and pineapple, which will be our output for this program. You will see that we imported two libraries: the ArrayList class and the List interface. This is needed because you are using the ArrayList and because you need to call the interface it relates to, in this case, the List.

### Creating a HashMap

As explained earlier, a HashMap is a map data structure that uses a hash function to map keys to values. HashMaps are often used because they are fast, flexible, and dynamic. Let's take a look at an example.

```java
import java.util.HashMap;//import relevant interface
import java.util.Map;//import relevant interface
public class HashMapExample {
```

```java
public static void main(String[] args) {

    Map<String, Integer> map = new HashMap<>(); // Create a new HashMap

    map.put("Apple", 5);// Add a single key-value pair using the put() method

    Map<String, Integer> fruits = new HashMap<>();

    fruits.put("Banana", 3);

    fruits.put("Orange", 2);

    map.putAll(fruits);

    //Add a single key-value pair using the add() method, return boolean indicating success or failure

    boolean added = map.putIfAbsent("Mango", 4) == null;

    if (added) {

        System.out.println("Mango added to the map");

    }

  }

}
```

In this case, our output will be "Mango added to the map" because we determined only that there was a banana with key value 3, an orange with key value 2, and apple with a key value 5.

However, we did not add a mango with key value 4, which the program identified, and because we placed a condition that if mango with key value 4 was absent, it should print "Mango added to the map," this is what happened.

## Adding Elements to a Collection

There are several different ways to add elements to a collection. Some of the most common methods include add(), addAll(), offer(), put(), and putAll(). For this example, we will use the same as the previous example, since I want to show you how you would add to it.

```java
import java.util.HashMap;

import java.util.Map;

public class HashMapExample {

public static void main(String[] args) {

Map<String, Integer> map = new HashMap<>();// Create a new HashMap

map.put("Apple", 5); // Add a single key-value pair using the put() method

// Add multiple key-value pairs using the putAll() method

Map<String, Integer> fruits = new HashMap<>();

fruits.put("Banana", 3);

fruits.put("Orange", 2);

map.putAll(fruits);

// Add a single key-value pair using the add() method, return boolean indicating success or failure

boolean added = map.putIfAbsent("Mango", 4) == null;

if (added) {

System.out.println("Mango added to the map");

}
```

```
// Add a single key-value pair using the offer() method

map.computeIfAbsent("Pineapple", k -> 6);

System.out.println(map);

}
}
```

The output, in this case, will be:

Mango added to the map

{Apple=5, Mango=4, Pineapple=6, Orange=2, Banana=3}

We have mapped here each of the keys that were related to each of the fruits and, differently from the previous example, we have now asked the system to add mango to the list according to the key by which it was identified. Therefore, the system is telling us that mango with key number 4 didn't previously exist on the list and that it was now added. It even goes a step further and tells us each of the fruits that are contained in the list and what is the key indicator related to each one of them.

### *Iterating Over a Collection*

There are several different ways to iterate over a collection. Some of the most common methods include for loop(), forEach(), iterator(), listIterator(), stream(). To exemplify how an iteration works in Java, I will reuse the code that showed what an ArrayList is.

```
import java.util.ArrayList;

import java.util.List;

import java.util.Iterator;

import java.util.ListIterator;
```

```java
import java.util.stream.Stream;
public class IterationExample {
public static void main(String[] args) {
List<String> fruits = new ArrayList<>();
fruits.add("Apple");
fruits.add("Banana");
fruits.add("Orange");
fruits.add("Mango");
fruits.add("Pineapple");
System.out.println("Iterating using for loop:");// Iterating using for loop
for (int i = 0; i < fruits.size(); i++) {
System.out.println(fruits.get(i));//placing getter
}
System.out.println("Iterating using for-each loop:");// Iterating using for-each loop
for (String fruit : fruits) {
System.out.println(fruit);
}
System.out.println("Iterating using Iterator:");// Iterating using Iterator
Iterator<String> iterator = fruits.iterator();
while (iterator.hasNext()) {
System.out.println(iterator.next());
}
System.out.println("Iterating using ListIterator:");// Iterating using ListIterator
ListIterator<String> listIterator = fruits.listIterator();
while (listIterator.hasNext()) {
```

```java
        System.out.println(listIterator.next());
        }
        // Iterating using ListIterator in reverse order
        System.out.println("Iterating using ListIterator in reverse order:");
        while (listIterator.hasPrevious()) {
        System.out.println(listIterator.previous());
        }
        System.out.println("Iterating using forEach() method:");// Iterating using forEach()
        fruits.forEach(fruit -> System.out.println(fruit));
        System.out.println("Iterating using Stream() method:");// Iterating using Stream()
        Stream<String> stream = fruits.stream();
        stream.forEach(fruit -> System.out.println(fruit));
    }
}
```

In the following example, we have used the methods for loop, for each, iterator, ListIterator, and Stream. Our output, in this example, will be:

**Iterating using for loop**:

Apple

Banana

Orange

Mango

Pineapple

**Iterating using for-each loop**:

Apple

Banana

Orange

Mango

Pineapple

**Iterating using Iterator**:

Apple

Banana

Orange

Mango

Pineapple

**Iterating using ListIterator**:

Apple

Banana

Orange

Mango

Pineapple

**Iterating using ListIterator in reverse order**:

Pineapple

Mango

Orange

Banana

Apple

**Iterating using forEach() method**:

Apple

Banana

Orange

Mango

Pineapple

**Iterating using Stream() method**:

Apple

Banana

Orange

Mango

Pineapple

**Observation**: Although the results I presented here do not show too much of a difference in a list of only five items, they will certainly be useful if you are speaking about longer lists with more information. It is also unlikely that you will use these methods as I have placed them here—I have only done so this way to exemplify all uses at once.

You should also take note that to use all these methods, I had to import all of the relevant packages into the program. If only one was missing from the list, our compiler would have pointed out an error.

Therefore, always ensure that you are referring to the correct library or libraries so that your code does not need to be fixed.

## *Removing Elements From a Collection*

There are several different ways to remove elements from a collection. Some of the most common methods include remove(), removeAll(), clear(), poll(), and take(). Let's use the same example as we did before to **remove** fruits from the list we created. One of the possibilities would be the following:

```java
import java.util.ArrayList;
import java.util.List;
import java.util.concurrent.LinkedBlockingQueue;
public class RemoveExample {
public static void main(String[] args) throws InterruptedException {
List<String> fruits = new ArrayList<>();
fruits.add("Apple");
fruits.add("Banana");
fruits.add("Orange");
fruits.add("Mango");
fruits.add("Pineapple");
// Removing a single element by value using remove() method
fruits.remove("Banana");
System.out.println(fruits);
// Removing multiple elements by value using removeAll() method
fruits.removeAll(List.of("Apple", "Mango"));
System.out.println(fruits);
// Removing all elements using clear() method
fruits.clear();
```

```java
System.out.println(fruits);
LinkedBlockingQueue<Integer> numbers = new LinkedBlockingQueue<>();
numbers.add(1);
numbers.add(2);
numbers.add(3);
// Removing a single element from the head of the queue using poll() method
int removedNumber = numbers.poll();
System.out.println("Removed: " + removedNumber);
System.out.println(numbers);
// Removing a single element from the head of the queue using take() method
int takenNumber =numbers.take();
System.out.println("Taken: " + takenNumber);
System.out.println(numbers);
    }
}
```

Here the output will be:

[Apple, Orange, Mango, Pineapple]: Because we removed **banana**

[Orange, Pineapple]: because we removed **apple** and **mango** and had previously moved **banana**.

[]: we cleared the list by using the removeAll() method

Removed: 1: because we added numbers and used the head of the queue using poll()

[2, 3]: because we added numbers and used the head of the queue using poll()

Taken: 2: because we asked how many numbers we removed

[3]: because it is the number that is left.

As you have seen, there are several possibilities on how to use each method in Java. There are so many options that it would make a very thick book if we were to list all of them and explain what they are and provide examples. In this section, I have shown you some of the most common collection uses while developing.

You will also see that I have also taken the opportunity to add some elements that we have seen in the previous chapters for easier reference. I believe that this way, you will be able to better understand the concepts of not only what I explained here, but also reinforce those we have seen in past chapters.

Although we will still see some practice examples at the end of this chapter, there is one final concept that is related to collections that I would like to teach you. It refers to what we call **autoboxing** and **unboxing** in Java. These are concepts that were added to Java in its 1.5 version because they felt the need to provide developers with the possibility of converting objects and primitive types to make reusability even more efficient when coding. Read on to learn more about what this is and how it can be useful when applied to your code.

## Autoboxing and Unboxing

**Autoboxing** and **unboxing** are actions in Java that are opposite to each other. While autoboxing is the automatic conversion of a primitive type to its corresponding object wrapper class, unboxing happens when an object wrapper class is converted back into a primitive type. The application of these concepts are important because they allow for increased flexibility when working with data structures. This process is usually carried out by the JVM and is used more commonly in collections.

One example where this could be applied is by using autoboxing to add primitive types to a collection. If you are thinking about the contrary, a useful application of unboxing could be to convert an object wrapper back into a primitive type when necessary.

**Pro tip**: While using autoboxing and unboxing can prove to be an advantage while coding, you should be careful when you use it. According to Study Tonight (n.d.), it can, sometimes, present unexpected results even while its main function is to prevent errors.

Read on to see an example of the application of these concepts to your code.

```java
import java.util.ArrayList;

import java.util.List;

public class Executor {

 public static void main(String[] args) {

int i = 5; // Autoboxing: int to Integer

Integer iWrapper = i; // Automatically boxed to Integer

Integer iWrapper2 = new Integer(5);// Unboxing: Integer to int

int i2 = iWrapper2; // Automatically unboxed to int

Integer iWrapper3 = new Integer(5);// Unboxing in method call

int i3 = doubleTheValue(

iWrapper3); // doubleTheValue method expects an int and unboxes the Integer

//You can also use autoboxing and unboxing in arithmetic operations and other expressions:

Integer a = 10;

Integer b = 20;

//Autoboxing and unboxing in arithmetic operations

Integer c = a + b; // a and b are unboxed, the result is boxed back to an Integer

// Autoboxing and unboxing in comparison operations

boolean isEqual = a == b; // a and b are unboxed and compared as int values

//Java also supports autoboxing and unboxing when working with collections, like List, Set, Map, etc.

List<Integer> numbers = new ArrayList<>();
```

```java
// Autoboxing when adding to the list
numbers.add(1); // 1 is automatically boxed to Integer
numbers.add(2);
// Unboxing when retrieving from the list
int firstNumber = numbers.get(0); // The Integer is automatically unboxed to int
}
public static int doubleTheValue(int x) {
return x * 2;
}
}
```

In this case, if you were to compile the code on your IDE, there would be no result, since we are not asking it to print anything—an error should not be shown either.

If you look at the example provided, you will see that we have autoboxed and unboxed int to Integer values in the code, as well as perform arithmetic operations with Integers turned into Int.

As you can see, this is a practical example of how Java provides the possibility to reuse the code. If you had, perhaps, used one of the objects before and needed to reuse it in another condition, you could simply apply the unboxing to change it accordingly.

The same is true for the reverse, when you could turn characters into numbers so they could be used in another part of your program that requires a calculation to be done, for example.

# Exercise

Now it is your turn! I have prepared four examples for you to practice the use of classes in Java. As usual, I will provide you with the text, the output, and a proposed solution to the problem. If you have any questions, don't be afraid to look them up in this or the previous chapters.

1. You work at an online grocery store and you need to remove the sold-out products without removing them from the code since you will have more of it in stock soon. How would you code this? For this example, use apple, banana, orange, mango, and pineapple as the products and banana and mango as the products that are sold out.

   The output should be: apple, orange, pineapple.

**Answer possibility**:

```
import java.util.ArrayList;
import java.util.List;
import java.util.concurrent.LinkedBlockingQueue;
public class Example {
public static void main(String[] args) {
List<String> products = new ArrayList<>();
products.add("Apple");
products.add("Banana");
products.add("Orange");
products.add("Mango");
products.add("Pineapple");
// sold out items
```

```java
List<String> soldOut = List.of("Banana", "Mango");
// remove the sold-out items from the products list
products.removeAll(soldOut);
System.out.println(products);
}
}
```

2. You work for a company that has online support through the chat feature. You need to create a program where the previous messages need to be removed from the system once they have been processed. How would you code this solution?

   For the messages, use Hello, How are you, and Goodbye.

   The output should be:

   Removed: Hello

   [How are you?, Goodbye]

**Answer possibility**:

```java
import java.util.Queue;
import java.util.concurrent.LinkedBlockingQueue;
public class Example {
public static void main(String[] args) {
Queue<String> messages = new LinkedBlockingQueue<>();
messages.add("Hello");
messages.add("How are you?");
messages.add("Goodbye");
// remove the first message from the queue
String removedMessage = messages.poll();
System.out.println("Removed: " + removedMessage);
```

```
System.out.println(messages);

}

}
```

3. You work for a website that provides several types of information to the public among which is the weather forecast in several cities in the United States. How would you add multiple cities to your code so that they are shown on the page?

   For this example, use the information contained on the following table:

   | City | Forecast (°F) |
   |---|---|
   | New York | 72 |
   | Los Angeles | 75 |
   | Chicago | 68 |
   | Houston | 82 |

   The output should be:

   {New York=72, Chicago=68, Los Angeles=75, Houston=82}

**Answer possibility:**

```
import java.util.HashMap;
import java.util.Map;
public class Example {
public static void main(String[] args) {
Map<String, Integer> forecast = new HashMap<>();
forecast.put("New York", 72);
forecast.put("Los Angeles", 75);
// new forecast data
Map<String, Integer> newData = new HashMap<>();
newData.put("Chicago", 68);
```

```java
newData.put("Houston", 82);
// add the new forecast data to the existing map
forecast.putAll(newData);
System.out.println(forecast);
 }
}
```

4. Suppose the company you work for has asked you to work on a task management application. Because of the demand and the actions that need to be completed, you need to add new tasks to a list in the order they will be performed. How would you code this?

    For this example, use: write report, prepare presentation, and attend meeting.

    The output should be:[Write report, Prepare presentation, Attend meeting]

**Answer possibility**:

```java
import java.util.Queue;
import java.util.concurrent.LinkedBlockingQueue;
public class Example {
public static void main(String[] args) {
Queue<String> tasks = new LinkedBlockingQueue<>();
tasks.offer("Write report");
tasks.offer("Prepare presentation");
// add a new task to the queue
tasks.offer("Attend meeting");
System.out.println(tasks);
 }
}
```

# Summary

In this chapter, you have seen how to use collections in Java and how they can be useful to make your code more efficient.

It will also make the development process easier without having to, for example, add and remove code every time you need to carry out a modification to your program.

However, we all know that when we are coding, we are subject to making mistakes. This is also true for the most experienced Java programmer.

In the next chapter, you will see what are some of the most common errors and exceptions to have while you are programming, the solution to them, and the alternatives you can apply when you see yourself facing one of them.

# Chapter 14: Troubleshooting, Debugging, and Handling Errors and Exceptions in Java

Being able to create a Java program is great. But if you don't know how to troubleshoot and debug Java programs, you will be unable to find and fix errors in your code. This can lead to wasted time, frustration, and even missed deadlines.

As ironic as it sounds, errors and exceptions are an important part of learning how to program in Java. They can be used to detect and fix problems in your code. When you start coding, it is more often than not to incorrectly name classes, mistake methods, and commit mistakes on the syntax you are using. It used to happen to me when I was starting and I am sure it will happen to you as well, especially as you progress in your knowledge. Both errors and exceptions in Java are part of a subclass named the java.lang.Throwable class.

The first thing you need to know to understand these concepts is the difference between an error and an exception. An **error** will generally occur when there is a problem in the environment and it cannot be solved with coding. This means that there is no mistake in the coding you have written, but rather in some other part of the program. There are three types of errors in Java: **Compile -(Syntax) Error**, **Runtime Error**, and **Logical Error**. An error is considered to be unrecoverable because it is part of the system and, once it is identified, the program will be forced to terminate..

On the other hand, an exception can be **checked** or **unchecked**. It generally occurs when there is an error in your code. They are fixable by going back to what you have written and manually fixing the problem or applying a solution that is called the try-catch block, which we will see further along in this chapter. When you have an exception, it can affect your program's flow. An exception can be recovered by making modifications to your code. According to Bhardwaj (2022), "An Exception can be thought of as a last line of defense to prevent errors."

In addition to this, Bhardwaj (2022) states that to think about it in a simpler way, you can use the following logic:

> An Error *indicates serious problems that a reasonable application should not try to catch*. Error is something you cannot predict, catch, or handle most of the time. It breaks your program's flow. A programmer wants to avoid as many errors as possible.
>
> On the other hand, an Exception *indicates conditions that a reasonable application might want to catch*. The exception was meant to give you an opportunity to do something with it, like try once more or try something else or write to the log. A programmer wants to handle as many exceptions as possible. (para. 29–30)

Therefore, one can say that it is better to catch an exception than an error since the first you can fix and the second can be hiding a deeper problem that you will need to identify and cannot be solved by coding. Now that you know the difference between these two problems that can appear while developing your software, let's take a closer look at the minor details each of them can present and examples of how they are presented when you run them through the compiler.

**Basic Errors and Exceptions**

Java has a standard set of errors and exceptions a developer can find while developing. First, they will either be an exception or an error. Next, if they are exceptions, they will be checked or unchecked and if they are mistakes, they will always be **unchecked** and will be one of these three: syntax error, runtime error, or logical error. Each of them refers to a different issue your program is facing and will need to be approached in its own particular way. In this section, I will give you the details on each of the exceptions and errors that can be found and what they mean to your development process.

*Exceptions*

Exceptions happen when you have a problem with your code that the program can catch while you are writing it. There are many reasons why an exception might appear when you try to run your code, but the positive aspect of them is that they are fully recoverable. If you look up the definition of an exception in Java, you will see that most of the sources will identify it as an abnormal condition or behavior that disables the program from working according to the expected flow. When you have an exception in your program, it can be either checked or unchecked, or **RuntimeException** and **IOException.**

When you identify an exception in your code, a useful approach is to be the most specific possible regarding the exception type, instead of catching a more general exception. When you act this way, it will make it easier to approach them in a more tailor-made manner and make it easier to solve the issues you are having.

**Checked**

A **checked exception** has this name because it can be verified, or checked, by the compiler when you try to run your program to see if it works.

**Unchecked**

Contrary to what a checked exception is, an **unchecked exception**, also known as a runtime exception, means that this cannot be identified by the compiler when you run your program. You will see more about what can cause unchecked exceptions in a little bit, under the "runtime errors" in this section. Most of the unchecked exceptions refer to runtime exceptions. These include when there are mistakes with objects, classes, methods, or dividing by zero, for example.

*Errors*

When you have an error, this can mean there is a problem with the resources you are using or that the JVM has a bug. These are usually known as problems that violate the rules of Java, such as forgetting to close a key at the end or forgetting to close parentheses in a method you created. Some of the examples that you can find when there is an error in your program include **OutOfMemoryError**, **StackOverflowError**, and **NoClassDefFoundError**. Let's see the three types of errors you can encounter while developing and what they would look like in code.

### Compile Time (Syntax Errors)

As the name might suggest, compile-time errors, or syntax errors, occur when there is a problem in the language you have used. These can include missing semicolons, misspelled words, using a class incorrectly, not invoking an argument, and many others. They will be identified by your compiler once you start running the code and the program will not run until you have fixed it. Suppose you have tried doing one of the examples I proposed before but there was an error that appeared in the compiler. If it was a syntax problem, you must correct the code line to make it work.

An example of a compile time error would be the following code:

```
public class StackOverflowErrorExample {
public static void main(String[] args) {
infiniteRecursion();
}
private static void infiniteRecursion() {
infiniteRecursion();
}
}
```

In this example, I used the infiniteRecursion() method and am calling it in an infinite loop. Because of this, the program will point to a StackOverflowError.

This error occurs when the stack (the memory area used to store method calls) runs out of space, which can happen when a method calls itself too many times, which is the case in this situation since it is being called on a loop. In the compiler, you will see the following message:

```
Exception in thread "main" java.lang.StackOverflowError
at StackOverflowErrorExample.infiniteRecursion(StackOverflowErrorExample.java:6)
at StackOverflowErrorExample.infiniteRecursion(StackOverflowErrorExample.java:6)
at StackOverflowErrorExample.infiniteRecursion(StackOverflowErrorExample.java:6)
// etc.
```

In this case, this is one of the examples where the error will not be possible to recover since it is a problem you have generated that is outside the control of the program. Another example, but of a recoverable error would be if you had the following code:

```
import java.util.Queue;
import java.util.concurrent.LinkedBlockingQueue;
public class Example {
public static void main(String[] args) {
Queue<String> tasks = new LinkedBlockingQueue<>();
tasks.ofer("Write report");
tasks.offer("Prepare presentation");
// add a new task to the queue
tasks.offer("Attend meeting");
System.out.println(tasks);
}
}
```

The compiler is showing me that the problem is:

/Example.java:6: error: cannot find symbol

tasks.ofer("Write report");

^

symbol: method ofer(String)

location: variable tasks of type Queue<String>

1 error

Can you identify what the problem is? As you can see, the compiler has told us where the issue is: There is a mistake in the tasks.ofer("Write report"); method. Now that I have highlighted it for you, it is possible to identify that there is a misspelling in the word "offer," since it is written only with one "f." In this case, if you correct the spelling and add the missing letter to the code, it will run.

Other compiler errors you can expect to see are:

- "expected," when there is something missing from the code;

- "illegal start of an expression," where there is a syntax error that disables the code from identifying what you want to do;

- "invalid method declaration; return type required," when you have incorrectly typed what the method is supposed to return; and

- "reached end of file while parsing," which generally means you have forgotten to add a curly brace at some point in the program (usually at the end to close the code block) (Stackify, 2021).

**Runtime**

Suppose you have finished running the code you wrote in the compiler and that no mistake was found. However, when you try to run the program in its environment, you keep getting a runtime error. This is a common error and also a difficult one to identify since it generally happens because the program is correctly executed but there is an error somewhere the compiler has not identified. This means that you will need to go back and check all the instances of your code to ensure where the problem has happened.

Some common examples of runtime errors can include:

- "NullPointerException," when a program tries to run a null object or an object without a value;
- "ArrayIndexOutOfBoundsException," which happens when the values of the array are not available; and
- "NoClassDefFoundError," when the file containing the class is not found in the main method or the file is not in the right directory (Stackify, 2021).

These errors are generally identified by the JVM.

One example of a runtime error is the following:

int[] arr = new int[5];

arr[10] = 100; // throws ArrayIndexOutOfBoundsException

In this example, the code we wrote is trying to store a value at index 10 of an array. However, as you can see the array was declared to have a size 5; therefore, 10 would be out of the bounds of the array causing an **ArrayIndexOutOfBoundsException**. This is an example of runtime error because it's caused by a problem within the program and it's not a checked exception, it doesn't need to be handled or propagated. Let's look at a different example.

String name = null;

System.out.println(name.length()); // throws NullPointerException

In this example, the code tries to access the length of a null String, causing a **NullPointerException** to be created. Once again, this will not be identified by the compiler, only when you run the program. The most common runtime errors occur when, according to Rollbar Editorial Team (2021), there are situations like:

- You try to perform a division by 0.
- There is the intent to access an element within an array that is outside the index declared number.

- The developer tries to store a type value to a collection that is not compatible with that format.

- There is an invalid argument in a method.

- Trying to convert an invalid string into a number.

- No memory space for the data.

**Logical**

Logical errors are the most difficult to identify. The reason for this is that they will not be caught by either the compiler or the program once it is running. This means that there is a problem in the design of your program or there is an issue in its implementation that will lead to unexpected behaviors by the program. This can be if you use logic that does not make sense but is accepted by the compiler or if a variable was incorrectly declared while writing your code.

Suppose you have asked the program to *divide* 25 by 5 so that the answer would be 5, but what you really wanted to do was to *multiply* the numbers, so that the result was 125. The operation is acceptable by the compiler and the JVM, but your output will result in a problem because you have added the incorrect command. In this case, this is entirely the responsibility of the developer or, in other words, a human mistake.

To identify a logical problem within your code, you can try several different techniques that go from asking someone to check it for you to using a debugging program. This will depend on the resources you have and what the error is. Since you are learning and can still be considered a junior developer, you might ask a more senior developer to take a look at what you did. Another approach is to use web-based communities and forums composed of developers from all over the world to obtain suggestions and answers to your problem. Getting a fresh perspective is, sometimes, the best way to continue forward and identify what needs to be improved.

## *Don't Stress If You Find an Error!*

As a part of your learning process, now that you know what each error and exception is, I suggest you go back to the previous examples you did and check if you can identify and fix them in your code attempts with the information I have given you. This will reinforce your learning and will enable you to see where you are making the most significant mistakes. My orientation is that you take notes and pay close attention to these since, as we move on to more complex subjects in the following chapters, you will see them being used in the coding examples I will provide.

Here, I would like to reinforce that errors are common when programming and it is nothing to be worried about. These bugs, as they are called, can be harder or easier to fix, but they should not define your career as a developer. As I mentioned earlier, even the most seasoned developer with years of experience makes mistakes and is prone to error. Take it easy on yourself; you are still learning! You will get it right if you practice.

In the meantime, while we haven't gotten there yet, I want to give you a few solutions on how to handle exception problems in Java and how to overcome potential problems. But first things first! Follow my suggestion and go back to the beginning of this book, test your codes, and see if you can debug them. After you have gone back and checked everything you created, come back to this section because the next thing I will teach you is how to *handle* exceptions in Java and avoid your program to bring you errors.

**Exception Handling Keywords in Java**

When you have runtime errors in Java, one of the best ways to approach them is to use exception handling. If you apply this approach in your program, it will enable you to have it carry its normal flow. In Java, there are five keywords that will help you handle exceptions when you embed them in the code. They are **try, catch, finally, throw,** and **throws**.

As you might remember from our keyword list from the beginning of the book, these words are there exactly because they are used when handling exceptions and, therefore, cannot be used in the code for any other purpose. Additionally, you can also create custom exception handling, as we will also see. Let's take a look at each of these words and what you can do with them.

**Java best practice**: Do not use handling exceptions throughout your code without criteria. You should use these only in special cases and not as an essential part of your code.

### Try

When we use the word **try**, we should add it to the beginning of a code block, since it will be used to specify the part of the code where we want the exception to be handled. However, since it is the beginning, it will also need an end to be appropriately used. Although it is usually associated with the word **catch**, you can also use **finally** with it to determine where the end of the exception is.

This is an example of what is known as the try-catch approach mentioned by Fadatare, (n.d.):

```
try {
// add here the code that may throw an exception
} catch (ExceptionType e) {
// add here the exception handling code
}
```

Above, you can see the general syntax of the try-catch expression. Let's see what it would look like in a real example when we try to perform an operation where we divide 10 by 0, which we know will give us a runtime error.

```
try{
```

```
divide(10,0);//the code that will give you an error
}catch(ArithmeticException e){//here you are writing what the exception is
System.out.println("Error: " + e.getMessage());//what you want the output to be
}
```

However, as I mentioned, we can also use it with the keyword **finally** as follows:

```
try {
// add here the code that may throw an exception
} catch (ExceptionType e) {
// add there the exception handling code
} finally {
// add here the code that will be executed regardless of exception
}
```

## *Catch*

The **catch** keyword is also another that cannot be used alone. It must always be used together with **try**. When developing, it can be your option to add **finally** to it or not. You can also use more than one catch in an expression when you are coding. Just as the use of try, it will be followed by opening and closing braces and putting the code between them. Since I have already given two examples in "try" that also use catch, I will now give you an example with the use of the keyword more than once adapted from Board Infinity (2022).

```
try {
// add the code that may throw an exception
} catch (ExceptionType1 e) {
// add the first exception handling code
```

```
} catch (ExceptionType2 e) {
//ass the second exception handling code
} finally {
//add the code that will be executed regardless of exception
}
```

## Finally

Thinking about how we use the word **finally** in real life will help you understand what it means in Java. When you use this keyword in your coding, it means that the code will need to be executed—it does not matter if there is an exception or not. Additionally, it will always follow a try-catch expression—it cannot be executed on its own. In the two previous sections, we have already seen the application of finally in a code and, therefore, I will not add an example here.

## Throw

When we use the keyword **throw** to handle an expression, it means exactly what it reads: that an exception will be thrown. You can use this expression for both unchecked and checked expressions. Let's take a look at an example:

```
class InvalidAgeException extends Exception {
public InvalidAgeException(String message) {
super(message);
}
}
void checkAge(int age) throws InvalidAgeException {
if (age < 0) {
```

throw new InvalidAgeException("Age cannot be negative");

}

}

In this example, the InvalidAgeException class is a specific customized class which was created to extend the Exception class. As you can see in the code, it adds a constructor that takes a message string as input; thus, providing more information on the message that, in this case, is that age cannot be negative.

## Throws

Lastly, we have the **throws** keyword that can be used when handling expressions. It will be used when the developer wants to declare an exception or, to put it in simple terms, to inform the program that an exception will occur. Unlike throw, we are not going to handle it. We are only going to add it to the method to state that it exists. If the developer wants to, they may add the throw keyword to handle the exception, although this is not mandatory. In an example adapted from Olson (2022), it would look like this:

public void divide(int a, int b) throws ArithmeticException {

if (b == 0) {

throw new ArithmeticException("Cannot divide by zero");

}

int result = a / b;

System.out.println(result);

}

In this example, I am asking the program to divide two integers established as input and divide them. However, as you can see, one of them is zero, so what I am asking it to do is to check if the second input (the divisor) is zero. Since it is, the method will throw an ArithmeticException with the message "Cannot divide by zero." In other words, what is happening here is that the method will not continue to execute after throwing the exception and it also will not be propagated to the calling method.

## One More Example

Now that you know all the words that can be used in handling expressions, let's see a code example where we use all the exception-handling keywords provided by Pankaj (2022b):

```java
import java.io.FileNotFoundException;
import java.io.IOException;
public class ExceptionHandling {
public static void main(String[] args) throws FileNotFoundException, IOException {
try {
testException(-5);
testException(-10);
} catch(FileNotFoundException e) {
e.printStackTrace();
} catch(IOException e) {
e.printStackTrace();
} finally {
System.out.println("Releasing resources");
}
testException(15);
}
public static void testException(int i) throws FileNotFoundException, IOException {
if (i < 0) {
```

```
FileNotFoundException myException =
new FileNotFoundException("Negative Integer " + i);
throw myException;
} else if (i > 10) {
throw new IOException("Only supported for index 0 to 10");
}
}
}
```

# Troubleshooting and Debugging Your Java Programs

When you think about IT terminology, it can sometimes be confusing. There are so many new words and information that we sometimes get lost in the middle of them all. While experienced developers can navigate them all with a certain calm that is to envy, when you are just beginning, these can be more difficult to understand until you get the hang of things.

Two words that are commonly used interchangeably but incorrectly are troubleshooting and debugging. You might have already heard these words and thought they mean the same thing. If it happened to you, don't worry, this also happened to me while I was learning (and I suppose it happens to most of us).

To start off, I want to bring you an interesting concept that will help you understand the differences between them that Putano (2018) used. According to him, "Programmers will spend more time debugging than with troubleshooting. However, their enhanced operational duties will cause them to troubleshoot more frequently" (para. 2). You might be asking yourself, *Why is that so? What is the difference between troubleshooting and debugging and are there any commonalities between them?*

## *Troubleshooting and Debugging Java Programs*

When thinking about **troubleshooting** and debugging, keep in mind the following: Troubleshooting is a general situation and debugging is a type of troubleshooting. When you troubleshoot, this can be done in any system and when I mean any, it *is* any. From your coffee machine, to the dishwasher, to the television, and your mobile phone—if it has a system, you can troubleshoot. This is the reason why troubleshooting is considered a general concept, it will essentially help identify the issues a system is going through and try to solve them.

On the other hand, if we are talking about **debugging**, we are not only talking about identifying a problem, but also we are trying to fix it at the same time. Since we are talking about electronic systems, you might be dealing with code and identifying where the problem is so they stop occurring. Therefore, when you think about these two concepts, you will understand what I cited earlier. Since you are dealing with code, you are more likely to spend more time debugging than troubleshooting, since you will be looking at the root cause of the problem in a system.

To ensure the best work is delivered, you need to debug your system before presenting it, deploying, or handing it over to another team. This will make you look more credible. Furthermore, if you find a bug in your code that you cannot solve, the best thing to do is to use a debugger or look for some help. You have already seen in this chapter the errors and exceptions that can happen to your software, so now it is a matter of studying and identifying what you are doing wrong so these mistakes stop happening.

I am confident when I say that knowing how to code is almost useless if you don't know how to fix the mistakes you are making. Debugging is an essential skill for you and to help others in your team. When you work with developing software, you are generally in what is called a *squad*, composed of more than one person from different areas, or even the client, who will look over what you are doing.

Because you are a team, more often than not, you will be asked to help find errors and fix mistakes. Being able to do so shows commitment and elevates your reputation (as long as you are not stuck-up about it or throwing people's mistakes on their faces, obviously).

Remember in the beginning of the book when I mentioned something called a **conditional breakpoint**? If you don't, I will refresh your mind: It is a feature in Eclipse, the IDE we have selected to use, that will enable you to add breakpoints to your code so that you can debug it by parts. This means that if you have a breakpoint and you run the program and a mistake is found, you will know that the error is inside that block, avoiding you having to look all over the potential hundreds of lines of code again.

Sometimes, we are so focused on coding and getting it right that we make silly mistakes. Leahy (2019b) names that some of the most common runtime errors include things like:

- single and double quotes that do not match or that are missing
- forgetting to add quotes when you are using a String
- using operators incorrectly or insufficient times
- failing to use the proper case in the word or forgetting to reference or create an object (remember, Java needs objects and it is case-sensitive!)
- not attributing a characteristic to an object

Additionally, if you can't find the solution to a problem, you can always consult the Oracle official documentation to understand how to troubleshoot or debug a code. The company's database provides several tips and helpful information that will aid you in determining what is wrong and how to solve it. However, apart from what is official, let's see what else you can do when you are trying to solve errors in your programs.

### *Tips for Troubleshooting and Debugging Java Programs*

Apart from using the conditional and exception breakpoints in your IDE, there are several other tools you can use to debug your program. The first might seem obvious, but many beginning developers seem to forget it: Test your code! You will need to constantly test your code, especially if you are starting off. This will save you (and your teammates) a lot of going back and forth and searching for where the mistake is.

One of the best ways to test the code if you cannot find the problem is to create other variations of it with examples so you can test. You read it right, I want you to reproduce the bug you found to see if you are able to solve it or not. If you can create a test where the problem is solved, this will mean that your code can be debugged.

However, if you try to reproduce it using other variables and the same error keeps appearing even after you have checked all the information, then I am sorry to say you will have to start over, because your code cannot be debugged.

You might want, for the previous example, to use a more scientific approach to the situation. Establish a hypothesis and work from it. Use all the variations and changes you can. *Think. Research.* If none of this seems to help, try asking someone to look it over for you. Ask for a second opinion. Write down your assumptions and work with them line by line.

Finally, one of the most obvious advantages of IDEs are that they have debugging tools that can help you. I know I should have said this before, but you were learning, you needed to practice it as it is. When you use an IDE, some of them will automatically correct the mistakes you make, such as forgetting a key at the end, for example.

This can be applied to most IDEs: Eclipse, NetBeans, Visual Studio Code, IntelliJ Idea, and so on. Furthermore, you even have packages in Java that will help you do this, such as the Java Debugger (JDB). You can use any of these tools to help you debug and identify what is going on with your code.

# Summary

In this chapter, you have learned all about the errors and exceptions in Java and how to treat them. You now know the difference not only between what is an error and what is an exception, but also what it means to troubleshoot and to debug a program. As you read, you were given examples on how each of these errors and exceptions behave and some efficient ways to take care of them.

You now know that exceptions can be checked or unchecked and that there are three types of errors that can be found in Java: compile time errors (syntax errors), runtime errors (also exceptions), and logical errors, the last which is the most difficult one to identify.

I want to reassure you that having to debug is no need to feel worried or that it is a terrible situation—to be an efficient developer, you will need to change your mindset about mistakes and accept that they happen and are a part of your development. Once you do, you will see that it will be much easier to take care of them by using any of the tools I have provided you.

Finally, whenever possible, remember to use an IDE to write your programs. It will help you fix problems faster and even correct some of them while you develop, increasing your productivity and reducing the time you will take to fix mistakes.

Now that you know all this, we are ready to go deeper into more complex themes in Java coding. Our first stop will be on learning how to create, write, and read files by using code. Although this is a very nice and important feature to know, you will see in the next chapter that it is one of the trickiest things you can learn how to do.

File handling in Java tends to bring the developer several mistakes because of the several lines of code it uses. Therefore, be sure that you have understood the concepts in the chapter and read on to enhance your knowledge!

# Chapter 15: Reading and Writing Files in Java

Java is a versatile programming language that allows developers to create a wide range of applications. One area where Java excels is in reading and writing files. Sometimes, however, working with files can be tricky. When you deal with Java, you will need to learn how to handle documents to create, read, and write these files—more specifically, learn in-and-out (I/O) methods. In this chapter, I will teach you how to carry out these tasks and manage your documents in Java.

## Introduction to Reading and Writing Files in Java

Much like most of the other tools in Java, there is a variety of libraries and packages you can use to read, write, and create files. This will basically depend on your preference and what you want to do with the file. For example, if just wanted to create a file, you would use the java.io package while if you wanted to create and write in it, the java.io.FileOutputStream is a better option since it does both actions at once, reducing the need to download two different libraries.

### Why Read and Write Files?

One of the main reasons you might need to read and write files in Java is because of the high volume of information some organizations work with. This might mean they need to work with file traffic, more specifically with moving information around the servers or between devices. When you are working with uploading and downloading documents, you are working with writing and reading, respectively.

Now, imagine in this internet-based era we live in, where most of our operations are carried out through a computer or a mobile device. You need to have systems that enable documents to be transferred online. Suppose you want to send an email to a friend with a picture attached. When you attach (or upload) the picture, you are *writing* or recording the information, and when your friend receives the information and downloads the file, they are *reading*.

### How to Read and Write Files in Java

To understand how to manage this information in Java, you will need to understand the concept of *stream*, which we have seen in Chapter 13 when we mentioned collections. To do a small recap, a stream is a sequence of data that can be either an input or an output. Shreyasnaphad (2022) mentions that in Java, there are six types of input streams that are used to read data from specific places.

Imagine this, when you are typing a document on your computer, it is receiving information from your keyboard or when you are downloading a file it is being saved in your computer. The subclasses of the InputStream class according to the author are:

1. AudioInputStream
2. ByteArrayInputStream
3. FileInputStream
4. FilterInputStream
5. StringBufferInputStream
6. ObjectInputStream

On the other hand, when you have the output, you need to consider things that are "coming out" as a result of your data input. This can be what is seen on your monitor, for example, as you type the text or the file that you are creating. This is called the OutputStream, whose classes are used to write the data. Shreyasnaphad (2022) cites they have other six classes:

1. ByteArrayOutputStream

2. FileOutputStream

3. StringBufferOutputStream

4. ObjectOutputStream

5. DataOutputStream

6. PrintStream

You will use the methods available in these classes such as read(), write(), mark(), and others to write the file you wish to create. Remember when I mentioned in the beginning that we could use several different packages to read and write files? In the example I will show you in a little bit, we are going to use the OutputStream class or the package that is called import java.io.FileOutputStream.

Other ways to write Java files include the FileWriter, the BufferedWriter, and the Files utility class. The option you choose will depend on the size of the file and text you are going to use and how much memory will be required to generate the document and write in it.

In addition to this, you have other methods that are native to Java and are usually used when writing and creating files. These include getName(), which will return the name of the file; canRead(), which will test if it is possible to read the file; and delete(), which deletes a file, as the name suggests.

Let's take a look at an example of how we can create and write a file in Java.

## Creating and Writing Files in Java

Since we are going to create and write a file in Java in this example, I will not use the File class (java.io.File), but rather the FileOutputStream, as previously mentioned. You will also need to import the java.io.IOException class to handle possible errors your code might have, as we saw in Chapter 14. In this example, what we want to do is create a .txt file with the name "example" that will either return the answer "File created and written successfully" or "An error occurred while writing to the file" if the program identifies an error.

Let's look at what the coding in this case would look like. As usual, I have commented on each of the code lines so you can better understand the reasoning behind each one and follow step-by-step what I have done.

```java
import java.io.FileOutputStream;//import packages
import java.io.IOException;//import packages
public class FileWritingExample {
 public static void main(String[] args) {
String fileName = "example.txt";//type of file you want to create
String content = "This is a sample text to write to a file.";//content you want in file
try {
// create a new file
FileOutputStream fos = new FileOutputStream(fileName);
// write the content to the file
fos.write(content.getBytes());
// close the FileOutputStream to save the changes to the file
fos.close();
System.out.println("File created and written successfully.");
} catch (IOException e) {
System.out.println("An error occurred while writing to the file.");
e.printStackTrace();
}
```

}

}

Output: File created and written successfully.

In this case, the code worked and you have successfully created and written the program. The expected behavior here would be for the program to open and save a file in the root directory of a project. If you can see this file, this means that the program has worked and that all is going according to plan.

However, if we were to change the name and indicate it to write in a directory, for example, and changed the name of the example to add one such as /tttt/example.txt, your output would be: "An error occurred while writing to the file with the errors it found accordingly while compiling the code."

Now, if you just want to create a simple file, you could use the java.io.File library to create it together with the java.io.IOException class. The code would look like this:

```java
import java.io.File;

import java.io.IOException;

public class CreateFile {

public static void main(String[] args) {

try {//to handle errors

File myObj = new File("myexample.doc");

if (myObj.createNewFile()) {//method we are applying—createNewFile

System.out.println("File created: " + myObj.getName());

} else {//what happens if there is an error

System.out.println("File already exists.");

}

} catch (IOException e) {

System.out.println("An error occurred.");
```

```
e.printStackTrace();
     }
   }
}
```

In this case, since we have successfully created the file, the output will be: "File created: myexample.doc." For this example, the createNewFile method was used. Note that in this case, the name of the method cannot be changed and that the name of the object remained "File." We also used an if conditional to give us the answer depending on whether it was possible or not to create the file.

## Reading Files in Java

Now, if your objective is to read a file in Java, one of the possibilities is to use the java.io.FileInputStream class. You will note, in the below example, that the process is similar to creating a write file, but with commands relating to what you want it to do. In this case, we are creating the same example.txt but we are going to *read* it and, thus, we need to use *input*.

One thing to keep in mind here is that we might possibly need to convert the characters so that the file can be written by the program we expect. To give you a real-life example, when you download a PDF onto your computer, it will generally ask what program you want to open it with. If you select Adobe Acrobat Reader, for example, the file will open.

However, if you select Excel, it probably won't open because it does not have the .xls or .csv format that Excel can read. Or, maybe if you received an attachment in your WhatsApp and deleted it, if you wanted to open it again, you would get an error message saying something similar to "This file does not exist."

Let's take a look at how this would look in code format.

```java
import java.io.FileInputStream;
import java.io.IOException;
public class FileReadingExample {
 public static void main(String[] args) {
String fileName = "example.txt";
try {
// open the file
FileInputStream fis = new FileInputStream(fileName);
// read the file's content into a byte array
byte[] fileContent = new byte[fis.available()];
fis.read(fileContent);
// convert the byte array to a string
String content = new String(fileContent);
System.out.println("File content: " + content);
// close the FileInputStream
fis.close();
} catch (IOException e) {
System.out.println("An error occurred while reading the file.");
e.printStackTrace();
}
}
}
```

Output: An error occurred while reading the file.

Now, are you able to tell me why this error occurred when we put it to run in the compiler? If you guessed that it is because the file does not exist on my computer, you are correct!

Suppose you tried it and you did not create the previous example on the "create and write" example. You would see the following message appear:

java.io.FileNotFoundException: example.txt (No such file or directory)

at java.base/java.io.FileInputStream.open0(Native Method)

at java.base/java.io.FileInputStream.open(FileInputStream.java:216)

at java.base/java.io.FileInputStream.<init>(FileInputStream.java:157)

at java.base/java.io.FileInputStream.<init>(FileInputStream.java:111)

at FileReadingExample.main(FileReadingExample.java:8)

If you look at the first sentence, you will see what the problem is: There is no file or directory in my computer with this name and, therefore, it cannot be read. If I did, however, there would be no error message and the output would have been: File content: This is a sample text to write to a file. (Note that for the reading example, I am supposing that we are going to read the file we created and wrote in the first example mentioned in this chapter.)

# Exercise

Create, read, and write a CSV file in Java. The file should be named example.csv. The file output should look as follows:

*File created and written successfully.*

| Name | Age | Gender |
|---|---|---|
| Charles Xavier | 30 | Male |
| Sue Storm | 25 | Female |
| Tony Stark | 35 | Male |

**Answer possibility:**

```java
import java.io.File;

import java.io.FileInputStream;

import java.io.FileNotFoundException;

import java.io.IOException;

import java.io.PrintWriter;

public class CSVExample {

public static void main(String[] args) {

String fileName = "example.csv";

String[] header = {"Name", "Age", "Gender"}; // declaring CSV header

String[][] data = {

{"Charles Xavier", "30", "Male"},

{"Sue Storm", "25", "Female"},

{"Tony Stark", "35", "Male"}
```

```java
}; // declaring data from CSV file
try {
    // create a new file and write the header and data
    PrintWriter writer = new PrintWriter(
    new File(fileName)); // creates a PrintWriter object to write to the file
    StringBuilder sb = new StringBuilder(); // creates a StringBuilder object to store the CSV data
    for (String h : header) {
        sb.append(h); // appends the current header value to the StringBuilder
        sb.append(","); // appends a comma as a delimiter
    }
    sb.deleteCharAt(sb.length() - 1); // removes the last comma
    sb.append("\n"); // adds a newline character
    for (String[] d : data) {
        for (String element : d) {
            sb.append(element); // appends the current data value to the StringBuilder
            sb.append(","); // appends a comma as a delimiter
        }
        sb.deleteCharAt(sb.length() - 1); // removes the last comma
        sb.append("\n"); // adds a newline character
    }
    writer.write(sb.toString()); // writes the CSV data to the file
    writer.close(); // closes the PrintWriter
    System.out.println("File created and written successfully.");
    // read the file's content
```

```
FileInputStream fis = new FileInputStream(
fileName); // creates a FileInputStream to read the file
byte[] buffer = new byte[fis.available()]; // creates a buffer to store the file's content
fis.read(buffer); // reads the file's content into the buffer
String content = new String(buffer); // converts the buffer to a string
System.out.println(content); // prints the file's content
fis.close(); // closes the FileInputStream
} catch (FileNotFoundException e) {
System.out.println("An error occurred while working with the CSV file.");
e.printStackTrace();
} catch (IOException e) {
System.out.println("An error occurred while reading the file.");
e.printStackTrace();
}
}
}
```

# Summary

In this chapter, you have learned the basics about handling files by using Java. You now know that it is possible to create several types of documents by coding and that there are several ways to do it. Although I have only approached two different ways of doing this, as you study and look for more references, you will eventually find the solution that best suits your needs.

Keep in mind that there is no one specific way to do it and that each developer will have their own approach to coding depending on their experience and the knowledge they have. The more you learn, the more resources you will have to choose the best option for your code. This chapter has brought you more advanced knowledge that will make it easy to integrate documents, whether they are uploads or downloads, into your programs and will be an extra added skill you will have.

It is time to take a step further into your education process by learning a more complex process in Java. In the next chapter, I will teach you how to create a database by using Java coding. This will be especially important if you are working with big data and large amounts of information you need to organize and filter for future use. The concepts we have learned in the previous chapter will all be applied, so keep an eye out for anything you recognize!

# Chapter 16: Using Databases in Java

Databases are a crucial part of many Java applications and knowing how to work with them is essential for any Java developer. One of the main applications of databases is in big data, one of the areas in which Java can be used. When you have a database, you are organizing your data in a way that it can be understood and electronically managed.

However, this does not mean that all databases need to have hard scientific information. Suppose you have a list of friends' addresses and phone numbers that you use to send a holiday card at the end of the year. This can be considered a database as well.

In this chapter, I will teach you everything you need to know about databases in Java, from creating them to manipulating data.

## How Databases Are Used in Java

Databases are very common today, and they can be seen from simple ecommerce to governmental archives. They can be used for several reasons, from organizing a large amount of information to providing easier access to it when there is too much data to sort out from. When we have a database approach to something, we can say that we have a Database Management System (DBMS). The DBMS is what enables the developer to work with databases and help them sort out the relevant information they need.

Knowing how to use a database is one of the top skills that a developer must have. One of the reasons is that "Database programming languages are one of the most demanding skills in the employment market one should be familiar with" (Code Institute, 2022). When we consider databases, we have some languages that are preferred, such as SQL, Python, and R.

However, the market is growing for Java developers who have this knowledge since companies want to associate their databases with the language they are already using in their programs. This will enable them to improve productivity and restrict access to certain information, for example.

Other advantages of using databases include having different ways to manage information, applying security rules, and having an easy way to backup and store relevant data. Apart from this, when you have a database, you are giving the data a relevant structure that will ensure that there is consistency, enabling you to see if there is any missing information within the fields and identify any problems there might be, such as repeated data.

## Creating a Database in Java

When you are considering creating or using a database in Java, the first thing you need to do is download the Java Database Connectivity (JDBC). This package in Java will enable you to connect, execute queries, and obtain results from the database you are creating. Next, you will need to decide what kind of database you want to use, and there are several to choose from, but you should try to use one that is object-oriented. For our example, we will be using the MySQL database, one of the most common in the market.

To use databases, you will also need to download the **java.io** and the **java.sql** packages to your computer. If you don't remember how to do this, please refer back to Chapter 1 where I have explained in detail how to do this.

The next step is essential, and it is to install the MySQL JDBC driver in your computer with a Windows Operating System by following these steps described in An Introduction to Java Database Programming (JDBC) by Examples With MySQL (Nanyang Technological University, n.d., Install MySQL JDBC DRIVER section):

1. Download the "latest" MySQL JDBC driver from http://dev.mysql.com/downloads ⇒ "Connector/J" ⇒ Connector/J 8.0.{xx}, where {xx} is the latest update number ⇒ In "Select Operating System," choose "Platform Independent" ⇒ ZIP Archive (e.g., "mysql-connector-java-8.0.{xx}.zip" ⇒ "No thanks, just start my download".

2. UNZIP (right-click and extract all) the download file into your project directory "C:\myWebProject".

3. Open the unzipped folder. Look for the JAR file "mysql-connector-java-8.0.{xx}.jar". The Absolute Full-path Filename for this JAR file is "C:\myWebProject\mysql-connector-java-8.0.{xx}\mysql-connector-java-8.0.{xx}.jar". Take note of this super-long filename that you will need later. COPY and SAVE in a scratch pad so that you can retrieve it later (item 2.3).

You have now connected your database to your Java program. Next, you will need to organize the information that you have in a way that the program will understand. Let's use the address and zip code example to set it up. We should have the following:

| Name | Address | Zip Code |
| --- | --- | --- |
| Bruce Wayne | 123, Bat Lane | 11234 |
| Diana Prince | 456, Amazon Avenue | 55678 |
| Clark Kent | 789, Flying Street | 00987 |

Next, according to the Developer.com Staff (2022), you should add the drivers to the $CLASSPATH of the application so that the Java application can find the drive manager of the system. Still, according to the article:

> To initialize the database driver, use the Class.forName() method, as shown in the code snippet below:

> Class.forName("com.mysql.cj.jdbc.Driver"); // to initialize mysql driver

> Once this is complete, you can go ahead and create a database connection. To do so, you need to create a connection object from either the DriverManager class or the DataSource class. The DriverManager class is easier to use.

> Connection con = DriverManager.getConnection(url, username, password); (How to Connect to a Database in Java section)

Your database is now connected and you are able to start working with it. You will use the information above to insert the information into the database as you would for any other part of your development process. Once the objects are created, you will be able to look for them using a set of commands that we will see in the next section, where I will explain how to use a simple database.

### *How to Use a Simple Database*

When you have a database in Java, the main advantage is to run queries through it to find information. This will be done by using query commands such as the **executeQuery**. By doing this, it will enable you to search for information that has been placed within the database and bring you fast answers.

### *Creating Tables and Fields in the Database*

Before talking about creating tables and fields in a database, I would like to make a separate note on the development and creation of databases. Although Java provides you with tools to upload files and information into the program, when you think about databases, you might want to think of them as a blank page where you will be creating your data.

This means that when you are creating a database from scratch, you will likely have to input all the information by hand. In this section, I will provide you with the method of creating tables and fields in the database and uploading them because it is essential to learn how to do this manually.

If your project is to create a database from nothing, you might be adding the information little by little as your Java database grows. You will then be able to export it to other formats by distributing it, as we will see in the following chapter. However, keep in mind that the database will likely be a "live" program, where you will need to constantly add and remove data as you go, especially if you are using one for ecommerce, for example.

To change this information, you will use the tools that have been given to you in the previous chapters.

Although it might sound disheartening that you will have to create and add item by item manually, if you think about it, and are just starting, this will be no problem and you will add the information as you go.

With further ado, let's take a look at a code example for creating a database in Java. One of the coding possibilities would be the following:

```java
import java.sql.*;

public class ShopListDB {

public static void main(String[] args) {

Connection conn = null;

Statement stmt = null;

try {

// Connect to the H2 in-memory database using the default URL

conn = DriverManager.getConnection("jdbc:h2:~/test", "sa", "");

// Create the shoplist table

stmt = conn.createStatement();

String sql = "CREATE TABLE shoplist (id INTEGER NOT NULL, item VARCHAR(255), quantity INTEGER, PRIMARY KEY (id))";

stmt.executeUpdate(sql);

System.out.println("Table created successfully");

} catch (SQLException se) {

//Handle errors for JDBC

se.printStackTrace();

} finally {

try {
```

```java
// Close the statement
if (stmt != null) {
stmt.close();
}
} catch (SQLException se2) {
// nothing we can do
}
try {
// Close the connection
if (conn != null) {
conn.close();
}
} catch (SQLException se) {
se.printStackTrace();
}
}
}
}
```

In this case, we have created a database that has a shopping list. Note that within the code, I have created the output "Table created successfully" to be printed when the database has been created. I have also added a few try and catch statements to handle possible exceptions that might be found. Now that your database is created, we should start adding some data to it. Let's see how this can be done.

### Inserting Data Into the Database

We will use the database we created to add an item to our shopping list. In this case, the index number of the item will be "1" as it is the first one, the item will be "apple," and we want to buy "10" units of the product. By using the previous database example, let's take a look at what the code would look like for adding these items.

```java
import java.sql.*;
public class H2InsertingExample {
public static void main(String[] args) {
Connection conn = null;
Statement stmt = null;
try {
// Connect to the H2 database
conn = DriverManager.getConnection("jdbc:h2:~/test", "sa", "");
// Create a statement
stmt = conn.createStatement();
// Execute a SQL statement to enter the lists you want to add to the list
String sql = "INSERT INTO shoplist (id, item, quantity) VALUES (1, 'Apple', 10)";
stmt.executeUpdate(sql);
System.out.println("Data inserted successfully");
} catch (SQLException se) {
se.printStackTrace();
} finally {
try {
if (stmt != null) {
stmt.close();
```

```
}
} catch (SQLException se2) {
// nothing we can do
}
try {
if (conn != null) {
conn.close();
}
} catch (SQLException se) {
se.printStackTrace();
}
}
}
}
```

According to the code, the items have been successfully added to the list! Way to go! Do you think you can add more items to the list and test the code to see if you have understood the concept? Try adding item 2—banana—with 5 units and let's see how it goes.

If you tried it and it worked, congratulations! You understood working with Java databases. If it did not, here is the solution that should have been done. You should add the following:

```
String sql2 = "INSERT INTO shoplist (id, item, quantity) VALUES (2, 'Banana', 5)";
stmt.executeUpdate(sql2)
```

And modify the apple variable to:

```
String sql1 = "INSERT INTO shoplist (id, item, quantity) VALUES (1, 'Apple', 10)";
stmt.executeUpdate(sql1);
```

The code above would then look like this:

```
String sql1 = "INSERT INTO shoplist (id, item, quantity) VALUES (1, 'Apple', 10)";
String sql2 = "INSERT INTO shoplist (id, item, quantity) VALUES (2, 'Banana', 5)";
stmt.executeUpdate(sql1);
stmt.executeUpdate(sql2);
```

As you have seen, we added another command line and numbered the SQL statement. If you were to add other items, you would do the same by adding 3, 4, 5, and so on.

## Advanced Database Concepts

When you think about databases, there are, of course, more things you can do in them than just executing queries and adding information. These are part of more advanced concepts, which include adding transactions to your data and indexing. These will be helpful, using ecommerce again as an example, if you need to update the quantity of products you have if you only sold a few. In this section, I will show you some coding examples of how to carry out these two actions based on the previous code that we used.

### *Transactions*

In this example, we will use some of the same information. We will start by connecting to the H2 in-memory database using the default URL, and then it creates a statement and executes a SQL statement to insert a new record into the "shoplist" table.

We will call the conn.commit() method to save the changes to the database and, if the commit is successful, it will print "Transaction committed successfully," otherwise, it will call the conn.rollback() method to undo the changes. As a result of the changes being unable to be carried out, the system should print "Transaction rolled back."

In this transaction example you will see, we will use the conn.setAutoCommit(false); // disable auto-commit mode statement for all the databases to be updated with the transaction you conduct. When you use AutoCommit, you are **automatically** confirming that you want all the information to be changed as per your instructions in the code.

This will be especially useful if you have one database for, for example, one database for sold items and one for your stock.

Once you update the sold items database, the stock database should also be automatically updated so that you do not have outdated information.

```java
import java.sql.*;

public class H2TransactionExample {
public static void main(String[] args) {
Connection conn = null;
Statement stmt = null;
try {
// Connect to the H2 database
conn = DriverManager.getConnection("jdbc:h2:~/test", "sa", "");
conn.setAutoCommit(false); // disable auto-commit mode
// Create a statement
stmt = conn.createStatement();
// Execute a SQL statement
String sql = "INSERT INTO shoplist (id, item, quantity) VALUES (1, 'Apple', 10)";
stmt.executeUpdate(sql);
// Save the changes
conn.commit();
System.out.println("Transaction committed successfully");
```

```java
} catch (SQLException se) {
se.printStackTrace();
try {
// If there is an error, rollback the transaction
conn.rollback();
System.out.println("Transaction rolled back");
} catch (SQLException e) {
e.printStackTrace();
}
} finally {
try {
if (stmt != null) {
stmt.close();
}
} catch (SQLException se2) {
// nothing we can do
}
try {
if (conn != null) {
conn.close();
}
} catch (SQLException se) {
se.printStackTrace();
}
}
```

}

}

**Pro tip**: Whenever you are inserting or changing the information, don't forget to add the command to save the modifications you have made or you will lose all of them. In the code above, this is expressed in the conn.commit(); statement.

## *Indexes*

When you add indexes to the database, this enables you to have enhanced performance and better use of the information. Baeldung (2020) supports this by saying that "the database index is a data structure that improves the speed of data retrieval operations on a table at the cost of additional writes and storage space" (@Index Annotation section). In the code example below, we will see how to create an index on a Java database.

```
import java.sql.Connection;
import java.sql.DriverManager;
import java.sql.SQLException;
import java.sql.Statement;
public class ShopListWithIndexDB {
public static void main(String[] args) {
Connection conn = null;
Statement stmt = null;
try {
// Connect to the H2 in-memory database using the default URL
conn = DriverManager.getConnection("jdbc:h2:~/test", "sa", "");
// Create an index on the shoplist table
String indexSql = "CREATE INDEX index_name ON shoplist (item)";
```

```java
stmt.executeUpdate(indexSql);
System.out.println("Index created successfully");
} catch (SQLException se) {
//Handle errors for JDBC
se.printStackTrace();
} finally {
try {
// Close the statement
if (stmt != null) {
stmt.close();
}
} catch (SQLException se2) {
// nothing we can do
}
try {
// Close the connection
if (conn != null) {
conn.close();
}
} catch (SQLException se) {
se.printStackTrace();
}
}
}
}
```

# Exercise

For the exercise in this section, I want you to create a database with the following characteristics:

The database will be a table of employees with ID number and name. In the class, you should create different methods to create the table, create an index, insert the data in the table, and recover the input data.

**Answer possibility:**

```java
import java.sql.*;
public class JDBCExample {
    // JDBC driver name and database URL
    static final String JDBC_DRIVER = "org.h2.Driver";
    static final String DB_URL = "jdbc:h2:~/test";
    // Database credentials
    static final String USER = "sa";
    static final String PASS = "";
    public static void main(String[] args) {
        Connection conn = null;
        Statement stmt = null;
        try {
            // Register JDBC driver
            Class.forName(JDBC_DRIVER);
            System.out.println("Connecting to database...");
            // Open a connection
            conn = DriverManager.getConnection(DB_URL, USER, PASS);
```

```java
createTable(conn);
createIndex(conn);
insertData(conn);
selectDataByIndex(conn);
} catch (SQLException se) {
 // Handle errors for JDBC
se.printStackTrace();
} catch (Exception e) {
 // Handle errors for Class.forName
e.printStackTrace();
} finally {
try {
if (stmt != null)
stmt.close();
} catch (SQLException se2) {
// nothing we can do
}
try {
if (conn != null)
conn.close();
} catch (SQLException se) {
se.printStackTrace();
}
}
}
```

```java
private static void createTable(Connection conn) throws SQLException {
    System.out.println("Creating table...");
    // create statement
    Statement stmt = conn.createStatement();
    // SQL statement for creating table
    String sql = "CREATE TABLE Employee (ID INT PRIMARY KEY, NAME VARCHAR(255))";
    // execute the statement
    stmt.executeUpdate(sql);
    // close statement
    stmt.close();
}

private static void createIndex(Connection conn) throws SQLException {
    System.out.println("Creating index...");
    // create statement
    Statement stmt = conn.createStatement();
    // SQL statement for creating index
    String sql = "CREATE INDEX idx_employee_name ON Employee (NAME)";
    // execute the statement
    stmt.executeUpdate(sql);
    // close statement
    stmt.close();
}

private static void insertData(Connection conn) throws SQLException {
    System.out.println("Inserting data into table...");
```

```java
// create statement
Statement stmt = conn.createStatement();
// SQL statement for inserting data
String sql = "INSERT INTO Employee (ID, NAME) VALUES (1, 'John Doe')";"
// execute the statement
stmt.executeUpdate(sql);
// close statement
stmt.close();
}
private static void selectDataByIndex(Connection conn) throws SQLException {
System.out.println("Selecting data by index...");
// create statement
Statement stmt = conn.createStatement();
// SQL statement for selecting data by index
String sql = "SELECT * FROM Employee WHERE NAME='John Doe'";
// execute the statement and retrieve the result set
ResultSet rs = stmt.executeQuery(sql);
// iterate over the result set and print out the data
while (rs.next()) {
int id = rs.getInt("ID");
String name = rs.getString("NAME");
System.out.println("ID: " + id + ", Name: " + name);
}
// close the result set
rs.close();
```

```
// close the statement
stmt.close();
    }
}
```

# Summary

You have now mastered the art of creating and managing databases in Java. If your idea is to create one to help with organizing data in your company, the instructions you have read in this chapter will help you to do it. From the basics of creating a database to performing complex processes with them, it will give you a starting point for developing better programs and providing information.

I want you to remember that the relevant packages always need to be downloaded and that you need to connect the database to your Java environment so that you can work with it. It is also important to remember to save the actions you conduct so the modifications can be stored.

You now have the basics of creating, modifying, and processing Java programs. What is left? Well, the last step I want to teach you is how to distribute your program to the final user. This will be the final part of the process that will need to be done once your program is ready, debugged, and tested. Continue to the next chapter to find out how this is done!

# Chapter 17: Distributing Your Java Applications

Throughout the past 16 chapters, you have been learning how to code and create programs in Java. Now that you already know how to code, you need to think about how you are going to make the application you created available to the final user or the client. This process is called **distribution**. To make the programs and applications that were created available to others, you need to know how to distribute them.

Because Java is one of the most popular programming languages in the world, there are many ways to distribute your Java applications. When you consider the best approach to do so, you will need to think about the client's parameters. To this effect, you should always have in mind the following, according to Frankel (2021):

> Distributing applications on a couple of computers inside the same company is not an issue. A lot of products are available for automating the pushing of files onto computers. Issues might start to appear when you need to coordinate the deployment across different physical sites. (para. 1)

To distribute your Java program, you will need to use the **jpackage** that is available in the JDK. This package will enable you to wrap up your program in a **JAR file**, which is how you will send your program to the final user. After you have generated and exported the JAR, you will need to ensure that the JRE is installed in the other machines that will use the program so that it can run. But first, you might be wondering why I am using the term *distribute* when referring to a Java program instead of *deploy*.

Well, this is for one very specific reason: Although they are interchangeably used by people who are not in the IT industry, this use is incorrect. In fact, distributing and deploying mean two different things if you speak to a professional. So, to eliminate the possibility of incorrectly using these terms, let's take a look at what each of these means.

## Distribution vs. Deployment

Although distribution and deployment are related, they are different concepts. Let's use a shopping example in the grocery store. Suppose you are done with your shopping (coding) and you are ready to pay. After you are done ensuring the products are within the expiration date (testing), you go to the registration machine and pay. The next thing you will need to do is put the groceries in a package so you can carry them (distribute). You will take the groceries home and place them in your cupboard. When you do this last step, you are deploying the groceries.

Therefore, what you can understand is that when you **distribute** a program, you are making it available for use by others by packaging the application and its dependencies so the final user can download it onto their machines and start using it. This so-called "package," as we will see in a little bit, can be an image, an executable file, or an installer, depending on how you decide to save it.

On the other hand, once you are done distributing the program, it will be ready for **deployment**, which means that the application will be ready to be installed and configured within the system, program, or application that it is intended to be used in. Because the package is "universal," you can use it on one machine or on many machines. Therefore, we can say that while the distribution will only depend on the developer who is preparing the program when you deploy it, it will be successful or not based on the available configurations.

## How to Package and Distribute a Java Program

When you are working on distributing a program, the first thing you need to do is what is known as **packaging** the code. This means that you will be grouping everything you have done and placing it in one single file to make it easier to deploy on another machine. This file will be saved as a JAR file and will be run on any machine or application that has a

JRE installed. Go back to the groceries example where I have described the packaging. This is exactly what you will do with your Java program, except that it will all be placed in one "bag" or file.

When you distribute the Java program, it is important to package it because it can be placed in the other machine or application as a single executable file instead of several smaller parts. This means that instead of having to carry each of the products you bound one by one to your car, you will be able to carry them at once. One of the things this does is improve the security of the process since all JAR files are digitally signed to enable authentication and the fact that it has not been modified to malicious content after it was packaged.

Another advantage of packaging your code into a JAR file is that it will significantly reduce the size of the final product. Imagine you have thousands of lines of code. This will make the program large and heavy to be transferred with compressing. Therefore, by packaging the code into a JAR file, you are also compressing it to make it easier, faster, and more user-friendly to execute. When the file is compressed, all you need to do to launch it is click twice on the file and it will immediately start to download to the intended destination.

But how do you package a code? In the following section, I will explain the process step by step using the first code you created: the "Hello World!" in Chapter 3.

### *How to Package My Code*

Java enables the developer to package their code in several different ways. One of them is the **java -jar** command that can be placed within the code lines after you are done. Suppose we have the following code:

```
package com.mycompany.projectone;
public class MyFirstClass {
public static void main (String[] args) {
System.out.println("Hello World!");
```

}

}

The first thing you will want to do is to **Save As** this file. Suppose that when we do this, we give it the name myexample.java. Click on save to save the program. Next, you will need to compile the program by using the **javac** command. When you do this, it will enable you to save all the .java files that are in the root directory of your computer. The command, in this case, will be **javac \*.java** (the word *javac*, a space, \*, a period, and the word *java*). In our case, we will be using: **javac -d.myexample.java**, which is how you will create the package.

The package "myexample" is now created. When you click on it on your IDE, you will see where it was saved. You will now prepare to put the package within the JAR file. It will include your compiled code and all the other necessary information the code for your program might need. To create the jar file, we will go to the current directory and type in **myexample.jar**, which will include all the class files available in the directory and in the resources directory. An example of the command would be as follows:

jar -cvfe myexamplejar MainClass \*.class -C src/main/resources

Now that the JAR file has been created, you are almost done to pass on the code to the final user. To test and run it, use the **java -jar** command so that the Main class can run and you can test if the packaging was correctly done. Once you have confirmed it, you are ready to go and send the code to the client for them to execute the code in their machines, or *deploy* it.

**Pro tip**: "To avoid naming conflicts packages are given names of the domain name of the company in reverse" (Hartman, 2020b, Packages - point to note section).

Although I have taught you one method of how to package a program in Java, you need to remember once more that there are several ways to do this according to what was established as a guideline by your organization and the customer. In addition to creating a JAR file, The Java Tutorials by Oracle (n.d.-e, Common JAR file operations section), the provider of the official documentation for the language, gives the following table for all the commands regarding Java operations as follows:

| Operation | Command |
| --- | --- |
| To create a JAR file | jar cf *jar-file input-file(s)* |
| To view the contents of a JAR file | jar tf *jar-file* |
| To extract the contents of a JAR file | jar xf *jar-file* |
| To extract specific files from a JAR file | jar xf *jar-file archived-file(s)* |
| To run an application packaged as a JAR file (requires the **Main-class** manifest header) | java -jar *app.jar* |
| To invoke an applet packaged as a JAR file | <applet code=AppletClassName.class archive="JarFileName.jar" width=width height=height> </applet> |

## How to Run a Java Program Once It's Been Distributed

You might have noticed that in the last line of the table, I showed you in the previous section, there is the mention of the word *applet* and you might be wondering what it is. No worries, I will explain it right now. A Java applet is simply when you have adapted your program for use in a web browser. Using this will enable you to test the code in a web browser before sending it off. The applet is also a Java class that is extended from the **java.applet.Applet** class (Tutorials Point, n.d.-a).

When you want to run an applet, you will need to have the JVM installed on your computer and extend the class within the code. If we apply it to our code, it would look like this:

```
Import.java.applet

Import java.awt

public class MyFirstClass extends Applet {

public static void main (String[] args) {

System.out.println("Hello World!");

}

}
```

Another option is to run your Java program as a standalone, which means that it will run independently. When you run a Java application as a standalone, you do not need anything to be installed in the target computer, such as libraries. The only thing you will need is the JRE. The main reason for this is that the JAR file will contain all the necessary information within it. To run the standalone program, you must use the command **java -jar myexample.jar** (note that I used the file name of my example, but you can adapt it to the file name you are using).

# Summary

This chapter has shown you what needs to be done after your code is ready to be used. You saw that the first thing that needs to be done is to package this program into a JAR file so it can be distributed.

After the distribution is done, you will be able to proceed with deploying the program to other users who have the JRE installed on their machines.

This was the last step of your Java program creation. Now that the process has come full circle, in the next chapter, I will provide you with some useful tips and refreshers for when you code using Java as my final piece of advice.

# Chapter 18: Tips and Tricks for Java Programming

Becoming an expert Java programmer takes time, practice, and dedication. But you can give yourself a good head start by getting a hold of all the tricks of the trade. Here are 50 of them:

1. Choose the right development environment.
2. Understand the difference between a JDK and a JRE.
3. Download the latest JDK.
4. Install the JDK.
5. Set up the PATH system variable.
6. Verify the installation.
7. Create your first Java program.
8. Compile and run your first Java program.
9. Learn the basic structure of a Java program.
10. Understand how comments work in Java.
11. Declare variables in Java.
12. Learn about the different data types in Java.
13. Perform arithmetic operations in Java.
14. Use the Java if statement.
15. Use the Java switch statement.
16. Use the Java while loop.
17. Use the Java for loop.

18. Learn about arrays in Java.

19. Use methods in Java.

20. Understand OOP in Java.

21. Create classes and objects in Java.

22. Understand inheritance in Java.

23. Use interfaces in Java.

24. Handle exceptions in Java.

25. Work with packages in Java.

26. Use the Java I/O package.

27. Serialize objects in Java.

28. Read and write files in Java.

29. Work with directories in Java.

30. Use the Java Date and Time API.

31. Format text using the Java MessageFormat class.

32. Localize your Java applications.

33. Use regular expressions in Java.

34. Generate documentation for your Java code.

35. Unit test your Java code.

36. Use a build tool such as Apache Maven.

37. Deploy your Java applications.

38. Use a Java application server.

39. Secure your Java applications.

40. Optimize your Java code.

41. Connect to a database using JDBC.

42. Use JavaServer Pages (JSP).

43. Use servlets in Java.

44. Use WebSocket programming in Java.

45. Use the JavaFX framework.

46. Develop desktop applications using Java.

47. Develop Android applications using Java.

48. Use Java 8 features such as lambdas and the stream API.

49. Use the new features in Java 9, 10, 11, and 12.

50. Be familiar with popular Java libraries and frameworks.

Congratulations on making it this far!

I hope that now, with the help of the information I have provided, you have all the necessary tools and skills to become a successful Java developer. With these final tips and reminders, you will be able to elaborate on a checklist to establish best practices for your coding process.

As you will see, some of these are directly linked to the chapters we have in this book, making it easier for you to go back and check the information if needed.

# Conclusion

Congratulations! You have finished your intensive training in Java programming and are now able to start writing your own programs! Throughout this book, you have learned basic steps such as preparing and configuring your environment, the main characteristics of Java, and how to write simple programs to more advanced concepts such as debugging your own codes, creating, reading, and writing files, and creating databases. Finally, you have also learned how to deploy and distribute what you have created for a functional program. Well done!

If you have practiced using the examples and exercises I have provided, you are more than ready to start looking for a job in the area. You should not feel discouraged about having so little experience—all of us started from somewhere to get where we are now. This is just the start of what I believe will be a very successful career as a developer for you. My suggestion is that you do not stop after reading this book: Keep practicing and searching for exercises where you can learn and develop the skills you have learned here.

Try setting up your own programs and projects. You can try using real-life data or imaginary information—it does not matter. The important thing is that you do not give up and continue the hard work. Consider joining GitHub, for example, and start posting your projects and ideas to get more visibility. You should keep the page organized and ensure that you showcase all your abilities. Some developers use this as a place to clear doubts, see ways they can enhance their programs, and share their knowledge with others; which brings me to the next suggestion you can make for this new career.

I want you to consider joining Java online communities where they are constantly talking about improvements in the language, suggesting packages and libraries, and providing all sorts of valuable information you, as a junior developer, will benefit from. As I mentioned in Chapter 14, getting to know more senior developers will help you not only with debugging and fixing errors in your code by providing a fresher perspective, but it will also bring you a networking value that will be essential when you start looking for a job.

Speaking of a job, you can now start updating your resume to start looking for a new position! Since you do not have any experience in the area, my suggestion is that you take these small programs and tests you generate for yourself to build a profile for yourself. The main reason for this is that during the interview process, you will likely be asked by the recruiter what your experience in Java is and how you would solve a certain problem.

If you have been practicing, these answers will come easier to you and you will certainly impress them! Knowing beforehand how to answer potential questions and being prepared will say a lot about you and what they can expect from your professional behavior.

In addition to this, be sure to look for some sample interview questions in different sources so you can brush up on your interview skills. If this is a career transition, you will also need to answer why you are changing areas and what attracts you to the coding world. You should try to be honest and clear in your intentions so they know you are taking this shift in careers seriously.

Last but not least, apply for all the jobs you believe fit your profile, and don't get upset if you receive a negative answer the first time. What you will need to do is keep up the work and build your profile. Good coding comes from practice—the more you do it, the better you will become. Insist on the search and you will see that little by little, you will improve your interview skills and expose your knowledge. Remember: Java developers are high in demand, so don't feel demotivated just yet—you will get there!

I would like to ask that if you think this book has helped you in any way, you let me know your thoughts by leaving a review on Amazon. This might help motivate others who are also trying to start or transition careers.

I wish you well and the best of luck in your new path with the new knowledge you have acquired.

# References

Agarwal, C., & Miglani, G. (2016, February 24). *Garbage collection in Java*. GeeksforGeeks. https://www.geeksforgeeks.org/garbage-collection-java/

Agarwal, H. (2019, July 8). *Variables in Java*. GeeksforGeeks. https://www.geeksforgeeks.org/variables-in-java/

Agarwal, P. (2017, February 28). *Comments in Java*. GeeksforGeeks. https://www.geeksforgeeks.org/comments-in-java/

Agrawal, S. (2016, November 7). *Data types in Java*. GeeksforGeeks. https://www.geeksforgeeks.org/data-types-in-java/

Arora, S. (2018, September 25). *Top 10 Java debugging tips*. Stackify. https://stackify.com/java-debugging-tips/

Asghar, A. (2022). *How to create an array in Java*. Linux Hint. https://linuxhint.com/create-array-java/

Baeldung. (2018, January 11). *Introduction to Java primitives*. https://www.baeldung.com/java-primitives

Baeldung. (2020, November 16). *Defining indexes in JPA*. https://www.baeldung.com/jpa-indexes

Beginners Book. (n.d.). *Java collections framework tutorials*. https://beginnersbook.com/java-collections-tutorials/

Bhardwaj, M. (2022, April 13). *Error vs exception in Java*. Scaler Topics. https://www.scaler.com/topics/java/error-vs-exception-in-java/

Bhatele, S. (2022, April 5). *Is Java still relevant in 2022?* Backend Developers. https://medium.com/backenders-club/is-java-still-relevant-in-2022-931d4bc4e49c

Board Infinity. (2022, November 10). *Exception handling in Java: How to use it*. https://www.boardinfinity.com/blog/exception-handling-in-java/

Chauhan, V. (2022, November 18). *Top 10 reasons to learn Java programming*. LinkedIn. https://www.linkedin.com/pulse/top-10-reasons-learn-java-programming-varuna-chauhan/

Cocca, G. (2022, May 2). *Programming paradigms – Paradigm examples for beginners*. FreeCodeCamp. https://www.freecodecamp.org/news/an-introduction-to-programming-paradigms/

Code Institute. (2022, January 18). *Database programming: An introduction*. https://codeinstitute.net/global/blog/database-programming/

Cyubahiro, P. (2022, April 18). *Object-oriented programming in Java – a Beginner's Guide*. FreeCodeCamp. https://www.freecodecamp.org/news/object-oriented-programming-concepts-java/

Das, P. (2022, January 15). *Common operations on Java collections*. Reflectoring. https://reflectoring.io/common-operations-on-java-collections/

Data Flair Team. (2018, January 30). *Decision making in Java (syntax & example)*. Data Flair. https://data-flair.training/blogs/decision-making-in-java/

Davidson, J. (2021, September 11). *A beginner's guide to using interfaces in Java*. MUO. https://www.makeuseof.com/using-interfaces-java/

Demit, A. (n.d.). *The real purpose of comments in code*. Cognizant. https://www.cognizantsoftvision.com/blog/never-use-comments-in-code-because-it-should-speak-for-itself-right/

Developer.com Staff. (2022, October 17). *How to use databases in Java*. Developer.com. https://www.developer.com/java/java-databases/

Devopscube. (2022, November 20). *List of open source Java build tools*. https://devopscube.com/list-of-popular-open-source-java-build-tools/

de Vries, H. (2020, February 29). *How does non-blocking IO work under the hood?* ING Blog. https://medium.com/ing-blog/how-does-non-blocking-io-work-under-the-hood-6299d2953c74

Doherty, E. (2020, April 15). *What is object oriented programming? OOP explained in depth*. Educative. https://www.educative.io/blog/object-oriented-programming

Downey, A., & Mayfield, C. (n.d.). *Recursive methods*. TrinkNet. https://books.trinket.io/thinkjava2/chapter8.html

Dubey, B. K. (2022, October 28). *Java extension methods*. GeeksforGeeks. https://www.geeksforgeeks.org/java-extension-methods/

Eclipse Foundation. (2022). *Eclipse Installer 2022-12 R*. https://www.eclipse.org/downloads/packages/installer

Edureka. (2019, August 19). *What are comments in Java? – Know its types*. https://www.edureka.co/blog/comments-in-java/

Every Answer. (2022, May 16). *What is the meaning of deploy in Java?* https://www.everyanswer.org/what-is-the-meaning-of-deploy-in-java/

Fadatare, R. (n.d.). *Exception handling keywords in Java*. Java Guides. https://www.javaguides.net/2018/08/exception-handling-keywords-in-java.html

Fendadis John. (n.d.). *Java variable declaration best practices*. Tutorials Point. https://www.tutorialspoint.com/Java-variable-declaration-best-practices

Frankel, N. (2021, February 14). *Distribution of JVM desktop applications*. A Java Geek. https://blog.frankel.ch/state-jvm-desktop-frameworks/6/

FreeCodeCamp. (2020, February 1). *Java interfaces explained with examples*. https://www.freecodecamp.org/news/java-interfaces-explained-with-examples/

Gauravmoney26. (2020, May 21). *Extends vs implements in Java*. GeeksforGeeks. https://www.geeksforgeeks.org/extends-vs-implements-in-java/

GeeksforGeeks. (2017a, February 6). *Setting up the environment in Java*. ttps://www.geeksforgeeks.org/setting-environment-java/

GeeksforGeeks. (2017b, March 23). *Inheritance in Java*. https://www.geeksforgeeks.org/inheritance-in-java/

GeeksforGeeks. (2019, January 2). *Functional programming paradigm*. https://www.geeksforgeeks.org/functional-programming-paradigm/

Glassdoor. (2022, September 15). *How much does a Java developer make?* https://www.glassdoor.com/Salaries/java-developer-salary-SRCH_KO0,14.htm

Great Learning. (2022a, August 2). *What is an instance variable in Java?* Syntax & More. Great Learning Blog. https://www.mygreatlearning.com/blog/instance-variable-in-java/

Great Learning. (2022b, September 21). *Type casting in Java*. Great Learning Blog. https://www.mygreatlearning.com/blog/type-casting-in-java/

Great Learning Team. (2021a, January 2). *OOPs concepts in Java | 2023*. Great Learning Blog. https://www.mygreatlearning.com/blog/oops-concepts-in-java/

Great Learning Team. (2021b, March 5). *Method overloading in Java with examples.* Great Learning Blog. https://www.mygreatlearning.com/blog/method-overloading-in-java/

Great Learning Team. (2021c, May 27). *Inheritance in Java and types of inheritance in Java.* GreatLearning Blog. https://www.mygreatlearning.com/blog/inheritance-in-java/#what-is-inheritance-in-java

Hartman, J. (2019, October 2). *OOPs concepts in Java with examples.* Guru99. https://www.guru99.com/java-oops-concept.html

Hartman, J. (2020a). *How to download and install Eclipse to run Java.* Guru 99. https://www.guru99.com/install-eclipse-java.html

Hartman, J. (2020b). *Packages in Java: How to create/import package.* Guru 99. https://www.guru99.com/java-packages.html

Hartman, J. (2020c, February 20). *Java variables and data types with example.* Guru 99. https://www.guru99.com/java-variables.html

Hartman, J. (2020d, March 16). *Java string manipulation: Functions and methods with example.* Guru 99. https://www.guru99.com/java-strings.html#4

Hartman, J. (2021). *What is interface in Java: How to implement interface with example.* Guru 99. https://www.guru99.com/java-interface.html

Hartman, J. (2022, December 31). *Encapsulation in Java OOPs with example.* Guru99. https://www.guru99.com/java-oops-encapsulation.html

Henke, M. (2018, November 13). *4 reasons why we need code comments.* Software Quality Blog. https://blog.submain.com/4-reasons-need-code-comments/

Himanshi. (2023, January 13). *Jump statements in Java.* Naukri Learning. https://www.naukri.com/learning/articles/jump-statements-in-java/

House, C. [@housecor]. (2013, November 13). *Code is like humor. When you \*have\* to explain it, it's bad.* [Tweet]. Twitter. https://twitter.com/housecor/status/400479246713229312?lang=en

Java Assignment Help. (2021, November 23). *Top benefits of databases that you should know.* https://www.javaassignmenthelp.com/blog/benefits-of-database/#benefits-of-databases

JavaTpoint. (2011a). *Encapsulation in Java.* https://www.javatpoint.com/encapsulation

JavaTpoint. (2011b). *Java inner class.* https://www.javatpoint.com/java-inner-class

JavaTpoint. (n.d.-a). *Java comments.* https://www.javatpoint.com/java-comments

JavaTpoint. (n.d.-b). *Java garbage collection.* https://www.javatpoint.com/Garbage-Collection

JavaTpoint. (n.d.-c). *Java string.* https://www.javatpoint.com/java-string

JavaTpoint. (n.d.-d). *Return statement in Java.* https://www.javatpoint.com/return-statement-in-java

JavaTpoint. (n.d.-e). *Types of inheritance in Java.* https://www.javatpoint.com/types-of-inheritance-in-java

Javinpaul. (2022, February 24). *9 tips to become a better Java programmer in 2022.* Java Revisited. https://medium.com/javarevisited/9-tips-to-become-a-better-java-programmer-cad4c9334cc1

Khattri, A. (2018, July 24). *Errors vs exceptions in Java.* GeeksforGeeks. https://www.geeksforgeeks.org/errors-v-s-exceptions-in-java/

Kiriati, A. (2019, March 13). *Five code comments you should stop writing - And one you should start.* FreeCodeCamp. https://www.freecodecamp.org/news/5-comments-you-should-stop-writing-and-1-you-should-start-4d66a367cd2c/

Kirloskar, M. (2020, August 21). *How to learn Java collections - A complete guide.* GeeksforGeeks. https://www.geeksforgeeks.org/how-to-learn-java-collections-a-complete-guide/

Knudsen, R. (2022, December 21). *10 Java variable scope best practices.* Climbtheladder.com. https://climbtheladder.com/10-java-variable-scope-best-practices/

Konstantin. (2022, March 24). *A Java developer's checklist: What a developer should know.* CodeGym. https://codegym.cc/groups/posts/524-a-java-developers-checklist-what-a-developer-should-know

Kovačević, A. (2022, February 17). *How to install Maven on Windows (step-by-step guide).* Phoenix NAP. https://phoenixnap.com/kb/install-maven-windows

Kukade, G. (2020, January 29). *Guide to control flow statements in Java.* Soshace. https://soshace.com/guide-to-control-flow-statements-in-java/

Kumar, K. (n.d.). *Java miscellaneous operators*. CS Fundamentals. https://cs-fundamentals.com/java-programming/java-miscellaneous-operators#java-member-access-operator

Kumar, S. (2021, November 17). *Control flow in Java*. OpenGenus IQ. https://iq.opengenus.org/flow-control-in-java/

Kumar, S. (n.d.). *Scope and lifetime of a variable in Java*. Learning Journal. https://www.learningjournal.guru/article/programming-in-java/scope-and-lifetime-of-a-variable/

Laura M. (2018, August 30). *How to code in Java: The complete Java for beginners guide*. BitDegree Tutorials. https://www.bitdegree.org/tutorials/how-to-code-in-java/

Leahy, P. (2018, September 21). *A quick guide to using naming conventions in Java*. ThoughtCo. https://www.thoughtco.com/using-java-naming-conventions-2034199

Leahy, P. (2019a, February 28). *How to create your first Java program*. ThoughtCo. https://www.thoughtco.com/creating-your-first-java-program-2034124

Leahy, P. (2019b, July 1). *Fix common runtime errors in Java with careful debugging*. ThoughtCo. https://www.thoughtco.com/common-runtime-error-2034021

Lenka, C. (2019a, November 20). *Java do-while loop with examples*. GeeksforGeeks. https://www.geeksforgeeks.org/java-do-while-loop-with-examples/

Lenka, C. (2019b, November 20). *Java for loop with examples*. GeeksforGeeks. https://www.geeksforgeeks.org/java-for-loop-with-examples/

McCullum, N. (2020, May 16). *How to write Java comments the right way*. Nick McCullum. https://www.nickmccullum.com/how-to-write-java-comments/

Miglani, G. (2017, February 7). *Classes and objects in Java*. GeeksforGeeks. https://www.geeksforgeeks.org/classes-objects-java/

Minh, N. H. (2019, August 7). *How to generate Javadoc in Eclipse*. Code Java. https://www.codejava.net/ides/eclipse/how-to-generate-javadoc-in-eclipse

Minh, N. H. (2020, March 11). *How to create, build and run a Java Hello World program with Eclipse*. Code Java. https://www.codejava.net/ides/eclipse/how-to-create-build-and-run-a-java-hello-world-program-with-eclipse

Mittal, S. (2022). *10 tips to become better Java developer in 2023*. Java Hungry. https://javahungry.blogspot.com/2020/09/how-to-become-better-java-developer.html

MKYoung. (2009, November 25). *How to install Maven on Windows*. Mkyong. https://mkyong.com/maven/how-to-install-maven-in-windows/

Monus, A. (2018, July 20). *Six OOP concepts in Java with examples*. Raygun Blog. https://raygun.com/blog/oop-concepts-java/

Nanyang Technological University. (n.d.). *An introduction to Java Database Programming (JDBC) by examples with MySQL*. https://www3.ntu.edu.sg/home/ehchua/programming/java/JDBC_Basic.html

Nehra, M. (2022, July 27). *Tips and tricks to finding mistakes in your Java code*. Decipher Zone. https://www.decipherzone.com/blog-detail/java-code

Norlander, B. (2019, June 5). *Stop writing code comments*. Medium. https://medium.com/@bpnorlander/stop-writing-code-comments-28fef5272752

Ojha, A. (2016, July 29). *Default methods in Java 8*. GeeksforGeeks. https://www.geeksforgeeks.org/default-methods-java/

Olson, K. (2022, September 23). *Exception handling - Preventing errors*. Kevin's Guides. https://kevinsguides.com/guides/code/java/javaintro/ch13-trycatch

Oracle. (2019). *Variables*. https://docs.oracle.com/javase/tutorial/java/nutsandbolts/variables.html

Oracle. (n.d.-a). *Code conventions for the Java programming language: Naming conventions*. https://www.oracle.com/java/technologies/javase/codeconventions-namingconventions.html

Oracle. (n.d.-b). *Expressions, statements, and blocks*. https://docs.oracle.com/javase/tutorial/java/nutsandbolts/expressions.html

Oracle. (n.d.-c). *Running a Java web start application*. https://docs.oracle.com/javase/tutorial/deployment/webstart/running.html

Oracle. (n.d.-d). *Strings*. https://docs.oracle.com/javase/tutorial/java/data/strings.html

Oracle. (n.d.-e). *Packaging programs in JAR files*. https://docs.oracle.com/javase/tutorial/deployment/jar/

Ouaknin Felsen, L. (2017, October 30). *Functional vs object-oriented vs procedural programming.* Medium. https://medium.com/@LiliOuakninFelsen/functional-vs-object-oriented-vs-procedural-programming-a3d4585557f3

Palic, D. (n.d.). *Data conversion in Java.* Xenovation. https://xenovation.com/blog/development/java/data-conversion-in-java

Pankaj. (2022a, August 3). *Collections in Java - Everything you must know.* Digital Ocean. https://www.digitalocean.com/community/tutorials/collections-in-java-tutorial

Pankaj. (2022b, August 3). *Exception handling in Java.* DigitalOcean. https://www.digitalocean.com/community/tutorials/exception-handling-in-java

Pankaj. (2022c, August 3). *Java write to file - 4 ways to write file in Java.* DigitalOcean. https://www.digitalocean.com/community/tutorials/java-write-to-file

Paul, J. (n.d.). *10 programming best practices to name variables, methods and class in Java.* Java Revisited. https://javarevisited.blogspot.com/2014/10/10-java-best-practices-to-name-variables-methods-classes-packages.html#axzz7p2v5ZrFl

Pedamkar, P. (2019, March 7). *Advantages of OOP.* EDUCBA. https://www.educba.com/advantages-of-oop/

Pedamkar, P. (2020, March 16). *Mutable vs immutable Javas.* Educba. https://www.educba.com/mutable-vs-immutable-java/

Popovic, O. (2019, September 6). *Java flow control: For and for-each loops.* Stack Abuse. https://stackabuse.com/java-flow-control-for-and-for-each-loops/

Prabhu, R. (2019, February 12). *Strings in Java.* GeeksforGeeks. https://www.geeksforgeeks.org/strings-in-java/

Programiz. (n.d.-a). *Java break Statement (with examples).* https://www.programiz.com/java-programming/break-statement

Programiz. (n.d.-b). *Java inheritance (with examples).* https://www.programiz.com/java-programming/inheritance

Programiz. (n.d.-c). *Java methods.* https://www.programiz.com/java-programming/methods

Programiz. (n.d.-d). *Java operators: Arithmetic, relational, logical and more.* https://www.programiz.com/java-programming/operators

Programiz. (n.d.-e). *Java string (with examples)*. https://www.programiz.com/java-programming/string

Putano, B. (2018, April 10). *Troubleshooting vs debugging: What's the difference & best practices*. Stackify. https://stackify.com/troubleshooting-vs-debugging-whats-the-difference-best-practices/

Puzhevich, V. (2020, October 27). *Eclipse IDE for Java Developers*. Scand. https://scand.com/company/blog/eclipse-ide-for-java-developers/

Rabelo, J. (2019). *What is Java object?* Techopedia. https://www.techopedia.com/definition/24339/java-object

Ravikiran A S, R. (2022a, September 27). *What is Java interface and why it's needed?* Simplilearn. https://www.simplilearn.com/tutorials/java-tutorial/java-interface

Ravikiran A S, R. (2022b, October 27). *Collections in Java and how to implement them?* Simplilearn. https://www.simplilearn.com/tutorials/java-tutorial/java-collection

Ravikiran A S, R. (2022c, October 28). *What is encapsulation in Java and how to implement it*. Simplilearn. https://www.simplilearn.com/tutorials/java-tutorial/java-encapsulation

Rawat, R. (2017, September 29). *Return keyword in Java*. GeeksforGeeks. https://www.geeksforgeeks.org/return-keyword-java/

Reddy Katamreddy, S. P. (2022, May 3). *10 steps to become an outstanding Java developer*. DZone. https://dzone.com/articles/10-things-become-outstanding

Rollbar. (2019, February 12). *How to debug Java errors*. https://rollbar.com/guides/java/how-to-debug-java-errors

Rollbar Editorial Team. (2021, July 29). *How to solve the most common runtime errors in Java*. Rollbar. https://rollbar.com/blog/most-common-java-runtime-errors/

RootStack. (2022, February 18). *Types of variables in Java*. https://rootstack.com/en/blog/java-variables

Scientech Easy. (2020, June 1). *Methods in Java | Types, method Signature, example*. https://www.scientecheasy.com/2020/06/java-methods.html/

Scientech Easy. (2020, June 5). *Errors in Java | Runtime, compile time errors*. https://www.scientecheasy.com/2020/06/errors-in-java.html/

Scott, A. (2021, June 3). *Why do we need interfaces in Java?* Geek Culture. https://medium.com/geekculture/why-do-we-need-interfaces-in-java-9a95ef57a156

Selawsky, J. (2021, March 10). *10 tips to help you stand out as a Java developer.* Medium. https://betterprogramming.pub/10-tips-to-help-you-stand-out-as-a-java-developer-9865516584ae

Shreyasnaphad. (2022, January 1). *File handling in Java.* GeeksforGeeks. https://www.geeksforgeeks.org/file-handling-in-java/

Shriram. (2021, October 21). *What are the advantages of object-oriented programming?* UpGrad Blog. https://www.upgrad.com/blog/what-are-the-advantages-of-object-oriented-programming/

Simplilearn. (2021, March 23). *An introduction to methods in Java with examples.* https://www.simplilearn.com/tutorials/java-tutorial/methods-in-java

Singh, C. (2013a, May 18). *How to compile and run your first Java program.* BeginnersBook. https://beginnersbook.com/2013/05/first-java-program/

Singh, C. (2013b, May 18). *Java arrays.* Beginner's Book. https://beginnersbook.com/2013/05/java-arrays/

Sinha, N. (2022, June 28). *Extends keyword in Java.* Scaler Topics. https://www.scaler.com/topics/extends-keyword-in-java/

Software Testing Help. (2022, December 5). *Eclipse IDE: Create and run your first Java project.* https://www.softwaretestinghelp.com/eclipse/eclipse-creating-your-first-project/

Spertus, E. (2021, December 23). *Best practices for writing code comments.* Stack Overflow Blog. https://stackoverflow.blog/2021/12/23/best-practices-for-writing-code-comments/

Stackify. (2021, May 28). *Java software errors: How to avoid 50 code issues in Java.* https://stackify.com/top-java-software-errors/

Statista. (2022, August 9). *Most used languages among software developers globally 2022.* https://www.statista.com/statistics/793628/worldwide-developer-survey-most-used-languages/

Study Tonight. (n.d.). *Java autoboxing and unboxing.* https://www.studytonight.com/java/autoboxing-unboxing-java.php

Sufiyan. (2022, May 10). *String in Java*. Scaler Topics. https://www.scaler.com/topics/java/string-in-java/

Swift. (n.d.). *Extensions — The swift programming language*. https://docs.swift.org/swift-book/LanguageGuide/Extensions.html

Techopedia. (2012, November 8). *What is array in Java?* https://www.techopedia.com/definition/1143/array-java

Techopedia. (2020, October 6). *What is Java Development Kit (JDK)?* https://www.techopedia.com/definition/5594/java-development-kit-jdk

TechTarget. (2016, July). *Java IDE*. The Server Side. https://www.theserverside.com/definition/Java-IDE

TechVidvan Team. (2020, February 17). *Decision making in Java - Explore the types of statements with syntax*. Tech Vidvan. https://techvidvan.com/tutorials/decision-making-in-java/

Thirunavukkarasu, N. (2018, March 25). *Java NIO(New I/O) vs. IO*. Medium. https://medium.com/@nilasini/java-nio-non-blocking-io-vs-io-1731caa910a2

Tutorials Point. (n.d.-a). *Applet basics*. https://www.tutorialspoint.com/java/java_applet_basics.htm

Tutorials Point. (n.d.-b). *Can I define more than one public class in a Java package?* https://www.tutorialspoint.com/can-i-define-more-than-one-public-class-in-a-java-package

Tutorials Point. (n.d.-c). *Continue statement in java*. https://www.tutorialspoint.com/java/java_continue_statement.htm

Tutorials Point. (n.d.-d). *Eclipse - Debugging program*. https://www.tutorialspoint.com/eclipse/eclipse_debugging_program.htm

Tutorials Point. (n.d.-e). *How to run a Java program*. https://www.tutorialspoint.com/How-to-run-a-java-program

Tutorials Point. (n.d.-f). *Java - Collections framework*. https://www.tutorialspoint.com/java/java_collections.htm

Veeraraghavan, S. (2022, November 29). *20 most popular programming languages to learn in 2023*. Simplilearn. https://www.simplilearn.com/best-programming-languages-start-learning-today-article

Vogel, L. (2021). *Using the Eclipse IDE for Java programming - Tutorial.* Vogella. https://www.vogella.com/tutorials/Eclipse/article.html#create-your-first-java-program

Vogel, L. (n.d.). *Java debugging with Eclipse - Tutorial.* Vogella. https://www.vogella.com/tutorials/EclipseDebugging/article.html

W3 Schools. (2019). *Java packages.* https://www.w3schools.com/java/java_packages.asp

W3 Schools. (2020). *Java methods.* https://www.w3schools.com/java/java_methods.asp

W3 Schools. (n.d.-a). *Java comments.* https://www.w3schools.com/java/java_comments.asp

W3 Schools. (n.d.-b). *Java decision making.* https://www.w3schools.in/java/decision-making

W3 Schools. (n.d.-c). *Java method overloading.* https://www.w3schools.com/java/java_methods_overloading.asp

W3 Schools. (n.d.-d). Java strings. https://www.w3schools.com/java/java_strings.asp

W3Techs. (2023). *Usage statistics and market share of Java for websites, January 2023.* https://w3techs.com/technologies/details/pl-java

Web Dev. (2019, July 23). *What kind of jobs can you get with Java programming training?* Tosbourn. https://tosbourn.com/java-programming-training/

Whitman College. (n.d.). *Variables and data types.* https://www.whitman.edu/mathematics/java_tutorial/java/nutsandbolts/vars.html

wikiHow. (2020, August 19). *How to set up a Java programming environment.* https://www.wikihow.com/Set-Up-a-Java-Programming-Environment

Xu, T. (2022, April 26). *How to choose between package managers: Maven, Gradle and More.* Built In. https://builtin.com/software-engineering-perspectives/package-managers

Printed in Great Britain
by Amazon